THE FOOD AND COOKING OF
THAILAND

THE FOOD AND COOKING OF
THAILAND

THE AUTHENTIC TASTE OF SOUTH-EAST ASIA:
125 EXOTIC RECIPES SHOWN IN 250 STUNNING PHOTOGRAPHS

Judy Bastyra
Becky Johnson

LORENZ BOOKS

This edition is published by Lorenz Books, an imprint of
Anness Publishing Ltd,
Hermes House,
88–89 Blackfriars Road,
London SE1 8HA
tel. 020 7401 2077; fax 020 7633 9499

www.lorenzbooks.com; www.annesspublishing.com

If you like the images in this book and would like to
investigate using them for publishing, promotions or
advertising, please visit our website
www.practicalpictures.com for more information.

UK agent: The Manning Partnership Ltd;
    tel. 01225 478444; fax 01225 478440;
    sales@manning-partnership.co.uk
UK distributor: Grantham Book Services Ltd;
    tel. 01476 541080; fax 01476 541061;
    orders@gbs.tbs-ltd.co.uk
North American agent/distributor: National Book
    Network; tel. 301 459 3366; fax 301 429 5746;
    www.nbnbooks.com
Australian agent/distributor: Pan Macmillan Australia;
    tel. 1300 135 113; fax 1300 135 103;
    customer.service@macmillan.com.au
New Zealand agent/distributor: David Bateman Ltd;
    tel. (09) 415 7664; fax (09) 415 8892

Publisher: Joanna Lorenz
Senior Managing Editor: Conor Kilgallon
Editor: Amy Christian
Recipes: Judy Bastyra and Becky Johnson
Food Stylist: Lucy McKelvie
Stylist: Helen Trent
Photography: Nicki Dowey
Production Controller: Don Campaniello

PUBLISHER'S NOTE
Although the advice and information in this book are
believed to be accurate and true at the time of going to
press, neither the authors nor the publisher can accept
any legal responsibility or liability for any errors or
omissions that may be made.

ETHICAL TRADING POLICY
At Anness Publishing we believe that business should
be conducted in an ethical and ecologically sustainable
way, with respect for the environment and a proper
regard to the replacement of the natural resources
we employ.

As a publisher, we use a lot of wood pulp to make
high-quality paper for printing, and that wood
commonly comes from spruce trees. We are therefore
currently growing more than 750,000 trees in three
Scottish forest plantations: Berrymoss (130
hectares/320 acres), West Touxhill (125 hectares/305
acres) and Deveron Forest (75 hectares/185 acres). The
forests we manage contain more than 3.5 times the
number of trees employed each year in making paper
for the books we manufacture.

Because of this ongoing ecological investment
programme, you, as our customer, can have the pleasure
and reassurance of knowing that a tree is being
cultivated on your behalf to naturally replace the
materials used to make the book you are holding.
Our forestry programme is run in accordance with the
UK Woodland Assurance Scheme (UKWAS) and will be
certified by the internationally recognized Forest
Stewardship Council (FSC). The FSC is a non-
government organization dedicated to promoting
responsible management of the world's forests.
Certification ensures forests are managed in an
environmentally sustainable and socially responsible
way. For further information about this scheme, go to
www.annesspublishing.com/trees

Recipes in this book previously appeared in *Thai Food
and Cooking* by Judy Bastyra and Becky Johnson.

NOTES
For all recipes, quantities are given in both
metric and imperial measures and, where
appropriate, in standard cups and spoons. Follow
one set of measures, but not a mixture, because
they are not interchangeable.

Standard spoon and cup measures are level.
1 tsp = 5ml, 1 tbsp = 15ml, 1 cup = 250ml/8fl
oz. Australian standard tablespoons are 20ml.
Australian readers should use 3 tsp in place of
1 tbsp for measuring small quantities.
American pints are 16fl oz/2 cups. American
readers should use 20fl oz/2.5 cups in place of
1 pint when measuring liquids.

Electric oven temperatures in this book are
for conventional ovens. When using a fan oven,
the temperature will probably need to be
reduced by about 10–20°C/20–40°F. Since
ovens vary, you should check with your
manufacturer's instruction book for guidance.

The nutritional analysis given for each recipe
is calculated per portion (i.e. serving or item),
unless otherwise stated. If the recipe gives a
range, such as Serves 4–6, then the nutritional
analysis will be for the smaller portion size,
i.e. 6 servings. Measurements for sodium do
not include salt added to taste.

Medium (US large) eggs are used unless
otherwise stated.

Front cover shows Tofu and Vegetable Thai
Curry – for recipe, see page 102.

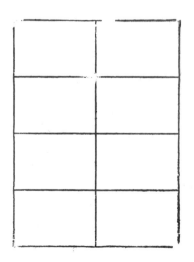

Contents

Introduction

For Thai people, food is an important feature of everyday life. Whatever the meal, whether it is a quick bowl of noodle soup bought from one of the many street vendors, or a meal shared at home with the rest of the family, eating is always a time for enjoyment.

Traditional Thai meals are generally an informal affair and there are no particular rules as to what time meals should be eaten. Food is separated into a savoury course and a sweet course, but within these categories the variety of dishes that make up the meal are served as soon as they are cooked. Family members and guests help themselves from the selection of dishes.

MAIN MEALS

Central to Thai cuisine is rice (khao). In fact, the Thai word "to eat" is actually *kin khao* (to eat rice). For breakfast Thais may eat khao tom, which is rice cooked in twice the normal amount of water, leaving it with a soft soup-like consistency. Small pieces of cooked chicken, pork or fish can be added to this rice dish, or it may be served plain with egg, salt fish and pickles. Lunch is generally a light meal of either noodles or fried rice. Dinner is the most substantial meal of the day. Steamed rice is generally served with clear soup (which may be eaten either at the beginning or end of the meal), a steamed dish, a fried dish, a salad and a spicy sauce. Condiments include crushed dried chilli, chopped fresh chilli, pickled garlic, cucumber, tomatoes and spring onions (scallions). Then follows fresh fruit and a Thai-style dessert.

Meals are usually eaten with a spoon and a fork. The fork is held in the left hand and is used to push food on to the spoon. The food is then conveyed to the mouth using the spoon. Chopsticks are only used when eating Chinese-style noodles.

STREET FOOD

Wherever you go in Thailand, you will come across the famously energetic food vendors who cook their dishes on the side of the street, on the rivers, and in markets. As with all Thai food, neighbouring countries have

BELOW: *Crunchy stir-fries have fantastic flavour and texture. Serve with either rice or noodles.*

ABOVE: *Roasted aubergine salad with shrimp and egg.*

ABOVE: *Peppers stuffed with red curry paste and fish sauce, typical Thai ingredients.*

ABOVE: *Pickled shallots, often used as a condiment with South-east Asian meals.*

influenced street food: rich sauces from Burma, fish and shellfish dishes from Malaysia, and charcuterie from Laos. Hawker food is renowned for its freshness and flavour and is part of the Thai way of life; it is eaten and enjoyed by everyone. Favourites include khao poot (corn); *salapao* – steamed rice flour dumplings stuffed with pork or a sweetened bean paste – and khanom jip, a steamed snack made from minced (ground) pork or shrimp wrapped in wonton skins.

Another quick bite is bah jang, a mixture of sticky rice and peanuts combined with pork, mushrooms, Chinese sausage or salty eggs all wrapped in banana leaves. North-eastern Thailand is well-known for its crunchy grasshoppers, grubworms, ant eggs and potent fermented fish, as well as more familiar fare such as gai

yang (chicken cooked over a charcoal brazier and accompanied by glutinous rice and green papaya salad) or khanom jin (noodles with spicy fish). Fresh sliced fruit can also be bought coated in sugar, salt or dried crushed chilli flakes.

MARKETS

Throughout Thailand, you will find loud, colourful and crowded markets, which sell everything from flowers and clothes to fresh produce and delicious snacks. The street food excels here with Thai men and women gossiping loudly while tucking into appetizing dishes. There is a huge array of fresh foods available, from plucked chickens, ready for cooking in front of you, to large bins filled to the brim with seafood, fished from Thailand's extensive coastline.

FESTIVALS AND CELEBRATION

All this abundance does not go unnoticed by the Thai people, who place great importance on giving thanks for the food that nature provides them with. Homage is paid, in particular, to rice because of its importance in the Thai diet. Festivals such as Bun Bung Fai and the rice-ploughing ceremony in Bangkok centre around planting, while the Sart Festival celebrates the harvest.

Fruit is also of great importance and is celebrated with fruit fairs countrywide. Indeed some fruits, such as the mango (mamuang), have religious significance.

The food culture of Thailand runs very deep, and this book will show you how to enjoy making the most of this delicious, fresh and colourful cuisine.

Soups, appetizers and snacks

In Thailand, soups are served throughout a meal, providing tastes and textures that complement or contrast with the other dishes. These soups can be served as a light lunch or as prelude to a dinner party. There are also recipes for snacks and appetizers such as Roasted Coconut Cashew Nuts, Corn Fritters and Firecrackers – in Thailand, these are served up hot and fresh by street vendors.

Northern squash soup

This recipe comes from northern Thailand. It is quite hearty, something of a cross between a soup and a stew. The banana flower is not essential, but it does add a unique and authentic flavour.

SERVES 4

1 butternut squash, about 300g/11oz

1 litre/1¾ pints/4 cups
    vegetable stock

90g/3½oz/scant 1 cup green beans,
    cut into 2.5cm/1in pieces

45g/1¾oz dried banana
    flower (optional)

15ml/1 tbsp Thai fish sauce

225g/8oz raw prawns (shrimp)

small bunch fresh basil

cooked rice, to serve

FOR THE CHILLI PASTE

115g/4oz shallots, sliced

10 drained bottled green peppercorns

1 small fresh green chilli, seeded and
    finely chopped

2.5ml/½ tsp shrimp paste

1 Peel the butternut squash and cut it in half. Scoop out the seeds with a teaspoon and discard, then cut the flesh into neat cubes. Set aside.

2 Make the chilli paste by pounding the shallots, peppercorns, chilli and shrimp paste together using a mortar and pestle or puréeing them in a spice blender.

3 Heat the stock gently in a large pan, then stir in the chilli paste. Add the squash, beans and banana flower, if using. Bring to the boil and cook for 15 minutes.

4 Add the fish sauce, prawns and basil. Bring to simmering point, then simmer for 3 minutes. Serve in warmed bowls, accompanied by rice.

Nutritional information per portion: Energy 67Kcal/284kJ; Protein 11.5g; Carbohydrate 3.6g, of which sugars 2.9g; Fat 0.9g, of which saturates 0.2g; Cholesterol 110mg; Calcium 82mg; Fibre 1.7g; Sodium 409mg.

Cellophane noodle soup

The noodles used in this soup go by various names: glass noodles, cellophane noodles, bean thread or transparent noodles. They are especially valued for their brittle texture.

SERVES 4

4 large dried shiitake mushrooms

15g/¹/₂oz dried lily buds

¹/₂ cucumber, coarsely chopped

2 garlic cloves, halved

90g/3¹/₂oz white cabbage, chopped

1.2 litres/2 pints/5 cups
    boiling water

115g/4oz cellophane noodles

30ml/2 tbsp soy sauce

15ml/1 tbsp palm sugar (jaggery) or
    light muscovado (brown) sugar

90g/3¹/₂oz block silken tofu, diced

fresh coriander (cilantro) leaves,
    to garnish

1 Soak the shiitake mushrooms in warm water for 30 minutes. In a separate bowl, soak the dried lily buds in warm water for 30 minutes.

2 Meanwhile put the cucumber, garlic and cabbage in a food processor and process to a smooth paste. Scrape the mixture into a large pan and add the water.

3 Bring to the boil, then reduce the heat and cook for 2 minutes, stirring occasionally.

4 Strain the mixture into another pan, return to a low heat and bring to simmering point.

5 Drain the lily buds, and rinse. Cut off hard ends. Add the buds to the stock with the noodles, soy sauce and sugar. Cook for 5 minutes more.

6 Strain the shiitake soaking liquid into the soup. Discard the shiitake stems. Slice the caps and place them and the tofu in four bowls. Pour the soup over, garnish and serve.

Nutritional information per portion: Energy 143Kcal/598kJ; Protein 4.1g; Carbohydrate 28.3g, of which sugars 4.7g; Fat 1.2g, of which saturates 0.1g; Cholesterol 0mg; Calcium 135mg; Fibre 0.9g; Sodium 8mg.

Smoked mackerel and tomato soup

All the ingredients for this unusual soup are cooked in a single pan, so it is quick and easy to prepare. Smoked mackerel gives a robust flavour, tempered by the lemon grass and tamarind.

SERVES 4

200g/7oz smoked mackerel fillets

4 tomatoes

1 litre/1¾ pints/4 cups
   vegetable stock

1 lemon grass stalk, finely chopped

5cm/2in piece fresh galangal, peeled
   and finely diced

4 shallots, finely chopped

2 garlic cloves, finely chopped

2.5ml/½ tsp dried chilli flakes

15ml/1 tbsp Thai fish sauce

5ml/1 tsp palm sugar (jaggery) or
   light muscovado (brown) sugar

45ml/3 tbsp thick tamarind juice,
   made by mixing tamarind paste
   with warm water

small bunch fresh chives or spring onions
   (scallions), to garnish

1 Prepare the smoked mackerel fillets. Remove and discard the skin, if necessary, then chop the flesh into large pieces. Remove any stray bones with your fingers or a pair of tweezers.

2 Cut the tomatoes in half, squeeze out most of the seeds with your fingers, then finely dice the flesh with a sharp knife. Set aside.

3 Pour the stock into a large pan and add the lemon grass, galangal, shallots and garlic. Bring to the boil, reduce the heat and simmer for 15 minutes.

4 Add the fish, tomatoes, chilli flakes, fish sauce, sugar and tamarind juice. Simmer for 4–5 minutes, until the fish and tomatoes are heated through. Serve garnished with chives or spring onions.

Nutritional information per portion: Energy 209Kcal/868kJ; Protein 10.3g; Carbohydrate 6.6g, of which sugars 6.5g; Fat 15.9g, of which saturates 3.2g; Cholesterol 53mg; Calcium 19mg; Fibre 0.8g; Sodium 681mg.

Mixed vegetable soup

In Thailand, this type of soup is usually made in large quantities and then reheated for consumption over several days. If you would like to do the same, double or treble the quantities.

SERVES 4

30ml/2 tbsp groundnut (peanut) oil

15ml/1 tbsp magic paste

90g/3¹/₂oz Savoy cabbage or
   Chinese leaves (Chinese cabbage),
   finely shredded

90g/3¹/₂oz mooli (daikon),
   finely diced

1 medium cauliflower,
   coarsely chopped

4 celery sticks, coarsely chopped

1.2 litres/2 pints/5 cups
   vegetable stock

130g/4¹/₂oz fried tofu, cut into
   2.5cm/1in cubes

5ml/1 tsp palm sugar (jaggery) or
   light muscovado (brown) sugar

45ml/3 tbsp light soy sauce

1 Heat the groundnut oil in a large, heavy pan or wok. Add the magic paste — a mixture of crushed garlic, white pepper and coriander (cilantro) found in Thai markets — and cook over a low heat, stirring frequently, until it gives off its aroma.

2 Add the shredded Savoy cabbage or Chinese leaves, mooli, cauliflower and celery. Pour in the vegetable stock, increase the heat to medium and bring to the boil, stirring occasionally. Gently stir in the tofu cubes.

3 Add the sugar and soy sauce. Reduce the heat and simmer for 15 minutes, until the vegetables are cooked and tender. Taste and add a little more soy sauce if needed. Serve hot.

Nutritional information per portion: Energy 134Kcal/554kJ; Protein 7.7g; Carbohydrate 7.5g, of which sugars 6.6g; Fat 8.2g, of which saturates 1.5g; Cholesterol 0mg; Calcium 220mg; Fibre 3g; Sodium 1044mg.

Pumpkin and coconut soup

The natural sweetness of the pumpkin is heightened by the addition of a little sugar in this lovely looking soup, but this is balanced by the chillies, shrimp paste and dried shrimp. Coconut cream blurs the boundaries of the flavours beautifully.

SERVES 4–6

450g/1lb pumpkin
2 garlic cloves, crushed
4 shallots, finely chopped
2.5ml/½ tsp shrimp paste
1 lemon grass stalk, chopped
2 fresh green chillies, seeded
15ml/1 tbsp dried shrimp, soaked
    for 10 minutes in warm water
    to cover
600ml/1 pint/2½ cups
    chicken stock

600ml/1 pint/2½ cups
    coconut cream
30ml/2 tbsp Thai fish sauce
5ml/1 tsp granulated (white) sugar
115g/4oz small cooked shelled
    prawns (shrimp)
salt and ground black pepper

TO GARNISH
2 fresh red chillies, seeded and thinly sliced
10–12 fresh basil leaves

1 Peel the pumpkin and cut it into quarters with a sharp knife. Scoop out the seeds with a teaspoon and discard. Cut the flesh into chunks about 2cm/¾in thick and set aside.

2 Put the garlic, shallots, shrimp paste, lemon grass, green chillies and salt to taste in a mortar. Drain the dried shrimp, discarding the liquid, and add to the mortar, then, using a pestle, grind the mixture into a paste. Alternatively, place all the ingredients in a food processor and process to a paste.

3 Bring the stock to the boil in a large pan. Add the ground paste and stir well to blend. Add the pumpkin chunks and bring to a simmer. Simmer for 10–15 minutes, or until the pumpkin is tender.

4 Stir in the coconut cream, then bring the soup back to simmering point. Do not let it boil. Add the fish sauce, sugar and ground black pepper to taste.

5 Add the prawns and cook for a further 2–3 minutes, until they are heated through. Serve in warm soup bowls, garnished with chillies and basil leaves.

Nutritional information per portion: Energy 77Kcal/328kJ; Protein 6.8g; Carbohydrate 10.9g, of which sugars 10.2g; Fat 1g, of which saturates 0.5g; Cholesterol 56mg; Calcium 104mg; Fibre 1.3g; Sodium 877mg.

Hot and sweet vegetable and tofu soup

An interesting combination of hot, sweet and sour flavours that makes for a soothing, nutritious soup. It takes only minutes to make.

SERVES 4

1.2 litres/2 pints/5 cups
   vegetable stock
5–10ml/1–2 tsp Thai red
   curry paste
2 kaffir lime leaves, torn
40g/1½oz/3 tbsp palm sugar (jaggery)
   or light muscovado (brown) sugar
30ml/2 tbsp soy sauce
juice of 1 lime
1 carrot, cut into thin batons
50g/2oz baby spinach leaves, any coarse
   stalks removed
225g/8oz block silken tofu, diced

1 Heat the stock in a large pan, then add the red curry paste. Stir constantly over a medium heat until the paste is blended in. Add the lime leaves, sugar and soy sauce and bring to the boil.

2 Add the lime juice and carrot to the pan. Reduce the heat and simmer for 5–10 minutes, until the carrot is tender. Place the spinach and tofu in serving bowls and pour the hot stock on top to serve.

Nutritional information per portion: Energy 103Kcal/434kJ; Protein 5.5g; Carbohydrate 13.3g, of which sugars 12.8g; Fat 3.5g, of which saturates 0.4g; Cholesterol 0mg; Calcium 320mg; Fibre 0.7g; Sodium 769mg.

Omelette soup

A very satisfying soup that is quick and easy to prepare. It is versatile, too, in that you can vary the vegetables according to what is available.

SERVES 4

1 egg
15ml/1 tbsp groundnut (peanut) oil
900ml/1¹/₂ pints/3³/₄ cups
    vegetable stock
2 large carrots, finely diced
4 outer leaves Savoy
    cabbage, shredded
30ml/2 tbsp soy sauce
2.5ml/¹/₂ tsp granulated (white) sugar
2.5ml/¹/₂ tsp ground black pepper
fresh coriander (cilantro) leaves,
    to garnish

1 Put the egg in a bowl and beat lightly with a fork.

2 Heat the oil in a small frying pan until hot, but not smoking. Pour in the egg and swirl the pan to coat the base evenly. Cook over a medium heat until set and the underside is golden. Slide out of the pan and roll up like a pancake. Slice into 5mm/¹/₄in rounds and set aside for the garnish.

3 Put the stock into a large pan. Add the carrots and cabbage and bring to the boil. Reduce the heat and simmer for 5 minutes, then add the soy sauce, granulated sugar and pepper.

4 Stir well, then pour into warmed bowls. Lay a few omelette rounds on the surface of each portion and complete the garnish with the coriander leaves.

Nutritional information per portion: Energy 68Kcal/283kJ; Protein 2.7g; Carbohydrate 3.9g, of which sugars 3.6g; Fat 4.7g, of which saturates 1g; Cholesterol 55mg; Calcium 28mg; Fibre 1.1g; Sodium 772mg.

Chiang Mai noodle soup

Nowadays a signature dish of the city of Chiang Mai, this delicious noodle soup originated in Burma. It is also the Thai equivalent of the famous Malaysian laksa.

SERVES 4–6

600ml/1 pint/2¹/₂ cups coconut milk
30ml/2 tbsp Thai red curry paste
5ml/1 tsp ground turmeric
450g/1lb chicken thighs, boned and cut
    into bitesize chunks
600ml/1 pint/2¹/₂ cups chicken stock
60ml/4 tbsp Thai fish sauce
15ml/1 tbsp dark soy sauce
juice of ¹/₂–1 lime
450g/1lb fresh egg noodles, blanched
    briefly in boiling water
salt and ground black pepper

TO GARNISH
3 spring onions (scallions), chopped
4 fresh red chillies, chopped
4 shallots, chopped
60ml/4 tbsp sliced pickled mustard
    leaves, rinsed
30ml/2 tbsp fried sliced garlic
coriander (cilantro) leaves
4–6 fried noodle nests (optional)

1 Pour one-third of the coconut milk into a large pan or wok. Bring to the boil over a medium heat, stirring frequently with a wooden spoon until the milk separates.

2 Add the curry paste and ground turmeric, stir to mix completely and cook until the mixture is fragrant.

3 Add the chunks of chicken and toss over the heat for about 2 minutes, making sure that they are thoroughly coated with the paste.

4 Add the remaining coconut milk, the chicken stock, fish sauce and soy sauce. Season with salt and pepper to taste. Bring to simmering point, stirring frequently, then lower the heat and cook gently for 7–10 minutes, until the chicken is cooked. Remove from the heat and stir in lime juice to taste.

5 Reheat the fresh egg noodles in boiling water, drain and divide among four to six warmed bowls. Divide the chunks of chicken among the bowls and ladle in the hot soup. Top each serving with spring onions, chillies, shallots, pickled mustard leaves, fried garlic, coriander leaves and a fried noodle nest, if using. Serve immediately.

Nutritional information per portion: Energy 606Kcal/2569kJ; Protein 39.5g; Carbohydrate 88.7g, of which sugars 10.1g; Fat 12.9g, of which saturates 3.7g; Cholesterol 135mg; Calcium 84mg; Fibre 3.3g; Sodium 1111mg.

Tung tong

Popularly called "gold bags", these crisp pastry purses have a coriander-flavoured filling based on water chestnuts and corn. They are the perfect vegetarian snack.

MAKES 18

18 spring roll wrappers, about
   8cm/3¼in square, thawed if frozen
vegetable oil, for deep-frying
plum sauce, to serve

FOR THE FILLING

4 baby corn cobs
130g/4½oz can water chestnuts,
   drained and chopped
1 shallot, coarsely chopped
1 egg, separated
30ml/2 tbsp cornflour (cornstarch)
60ml/4 tbsp water
small bunch fresh coriander
   (cilantro), chopped
salt and ground black pepper

1 Make the filling. Place the corn, water chestnuts, shallot and egg yolk in a food processor or blender. Process to a coarse paste. Place the egg white in a cup and whisk lightly with a fork. Put the cornflour in a small pan and stir in the water until smooth. Add the corn mixture and coriander and season to taste. Cook over a low heat, stirring constantly, until thickened.

2 Leave the filling to cool slightly, then place 5ml/1 tsp in the centre of a spring roll wrapper. Brush the edges with the beaten egg white, then gather up the points and press them firmly together to make a pouch or bag. Repeat with the remaining wrappers and filling.

3 Heat the oil in a large pan, deep-fryer or wok to 190°C/375°F or until a cube of bread, added to the oil, browns in about 45 seconds. Fry the bags, in batches, for about 5 minutes, until golden brown. Drain on kitchen paper and serve hot, with the plum sauce.

Nutritional information per portion: Energy 113Kcal/471kJ; Protein 1.6g; Carbohydrate 13.4g, of which sugars 0.7g; Fat 6.2g, of which saturates 0.9g; Cholesterol 11mg; Calcium 21mg; Fibre 0.7g; Sodium 55mg.

Stuffed Thai omelettes

Thai food often cleverly combines hot chilli with sweet flavours, as in the filling for these omelettes. It makes an interesting contrast to the delicate flavour of the egg.

SERVES 4

30ml/2 tbsp groundnut
    (peanut) oil
2 garlic cloves, finely chopped
1 small onion, finely chopped
225g/8oz minced (ground) pork
30ml/2 tbsp Thai fish sauce
5ml/1 tsp granulated (white) sugar
2 tomatoes, peeled and chopped
15ml/1 tbsp chopped fresh
    coriander (cilantro)
ground black pepper
fresh coriander (cilantro) sprigs and
    sliced fresh red chillies, to garnish

FOR THE OMELETTES
5 eggs
15ml/1 tbsp Thai fish sauce
30ml/2 tbsp groundnut (peanut) oil

1 Heat the oil in a wok or frying pan, add the garlic and onion, and cook over a medium heat, stirring occasionally, for 3–4 minutes, until soft. Add the pork and cook for about 8 minutes, stirring frequently, until lightly browned.

2 Stir in the Thai fish sauce, sugar and tomatoes, season with pepper and simmer over a low heat until slightly thickened. Mix in the coriander. Remove the wok from the heat, cover and set aside while you make the omelettes.

3 To make the omelettes, put the eggs and Thai fish sauce in a bowl and beat together lightly with a fork. Heat 15ml/1 tbsp of the oil in an omelette pan or wok over a medium heat. When the oil is very hot, but not smoking, add half the egg mixture and tilt the pan to spread into a thin layer over the base. Cook over a medium heat until just set and the underside is golden.

4 Spoon half the filling into the centre of the omelette. Fold into a neat square parcel by bringing the opposite sides of the omelette towards each other. Slide the parcel on to a serving dish, folded side down. Make another omelette parcel in the same way. Garnish with the coriander sprigs and chillies. Cut each omelette in half to serve.

Nutritional information per portion: Energy 303Kcal/1258kJ; Protein 19.8g; Carbohydrate 1.4g, of which sugars 1g; Fat 24.3g, of which saturates 6.4g; Cholesterol 303mg; Calcium 48mg; Fibre 0.2g; Sodium 314mg.

Chicken kebabs with satay sauce

These miniature kebabs are popular all over South-east Asia, and they are especially delicious when cooked on a barbecue. The peanut dipping sauce makes a perfect accompaniment for the marinated chicken.

SERVES 4

4 skinless, boneless chicken
   breast portions

FOR THE MARINADE
2 garlic cloves, crushed
2.5cm/1in piece fresh root ginger,
   finely grated
10ml/2 tsp Thai fish sauce
30ml/2 tbsp light soy sauce
15ml/1 tbsp clear honey

FOR THE SATAY SAUCE
90ml/6 tbsp crunchy peanut butter
1 fresh red chilli, seeded and
   finely chopped
juice of 1 lime
60ml/4 tbsp coconut milk
salt

1 First, make the satay sauce. Put all the ingredients in a food processor or blender. Process until smooth, then check the seasoning and add more salt or lime juice if necessary. Spoon the sauce into a bowl, cover with clear film (plastic wrap) and set aside.

2 Using a sharp knife, slice each chicken breast portion into four long strips. Put all the marinade ingredients in a large bowl and mix well, then add the chicken strips and toss together until thoroughly coated. Cover and leave for at least 30 minutes in the refrigerator to marinate.

3 Meanwhile, soak 16 wooden satay sticks or kebab skewers in water for 30 minutes, to prevent them from burning during cooking.

4 Preheat the grill (broiler) to high. Drain the satay sticks or skewers. Drain the chicken strips. Thread one strip of the chicken on to each satay stick or skewer. Grill (broil) for 3 minutes on each side, or until the chicken is golden brown and cooked through. Serve immediately with the sauce.

Nutritional information per portion: Energy 375Kcal/1564kJ; Protein 42.9g; Carbohydrate 3.9g, of which sugars 2.4g; Fat 20.9g, of which saturates 5.6g; Cholesterol 149mg; Calcium 27mg; Fibre 1.3g; Sodium 249mg.

Crisp-fried crab claws

Crab claws are readily available from the freezer cabinet of many Asian stores and supermarkets. Thaw them thoroughly and dry on kitchen paper before coating them.

SERVES 4

50g/2oz/$\frac{1}{3}$ cup rice flour
15ml/1 tbsp cornflour (cornstarch)
2.5ml/$\frac{1}{2}$ tsp granulated (white) sugar
1 egg
60ml/4 tbsp cold water
1 lemon grass stalk, root trimmed
2 garlic cloves, finely chopped
15ml/1 tbsp chopped fresh
    coriander (cilantro)
1–2 fresh red chillies, seeded and finely chopped
5ml/1 tsp Thai fish sauce
vegetable oil, for deep-frying

12 half-shelled crab claws, thawed
    if frozen
ground black pepper

FOR THE CHILLI VINEGAR DIP

45ml/3 tbsp granulated (white) sugar
120ml/4fl oz/$\frac{1}{2}$ cup water
120ml/4fl oz/$\frac{1}{2}$ cup red
    wine vinegar
15ml/1 tbsp Thai fish sauce
2–4 fresh red chillies, seeded
    and chopped

1 First make the chilli vinegar dip. Mix the sugar and water in a pan. Heat gently, stirring, until the sugar has dissolved, then bring to the boil. Lower the heat and simmer for 7 minutes. Stir in the rest of the ingredients, pour into a serving bowl and set aside.

2 Combine the rice flour, cornflour and sugar in a bowl. Beat the egg with the cold water, then stir the egg and water mixture into the flour mixture and beat well until it forms a light batter.

3 Cut off the lower 5cm/2in of the lemon grass stalk and chop it finely. Add the chopped lemon grass to the batter, with the garlic, coriander, red chillies and fish sauce. Stir in pepper to taste.

4 Heat the oil in a large pan, deep-fryer or wok to 190°C/375°F or until a cube of bread browns in 45 seconds. Dip the crab claws into the batter, then fry, in batches, until golden. Serve with the dip.

Nutritional information per portion: Energy 360Kcal/1500kJ; Protein 13.7g; Carbohydrate 26.7g, of which sugars 9.8g; Fat 22.3g, of which saturates 2.9g; Cholesterol 98mg; Calcium 90mg; Fibre 0.3g; Sodium 711mg.

Prawn and sesame toasts

These toast triangles are ideal for serving with pre-dinner drinks and are always a favourite hot snack at parties. They are surprisingly easy to prepare and can be cooked in just a few minutes.

SERVES 4

225g/8oz peeled raw prawns (shrimp)
15ml/1 tbsp sherry
15ml/1 tbsp soy sauce
30ml/2 tbsp cornflour (cornstarch)
2 egg whites
4 slices white bread
115g/4oz/1/2 cup sesame seeds
vegetable oil, for deep-frying
sweet chilli sauce,
   to serve

1 Process the prawns, sherry, soy sauce and cornflour in a food processor.

2 In a grease-free bowl, whisk the egg whites until stiff. Fold them into the prawn and cornflour mixture.

3 Cut each slice of bread into four triangular quarters. Spread out the sesame seeds on a large plate. Spread the prawn paste over one side of each bread triangle, then press the coated sides into the sesame seeds so that they stick and cover the prawn paste.

4 Heat the oil in a large pan, wok or deep-fryer, to 190°C/375°F or until a cube of bread, added to the oil, browns in about 45 seconds. Add the toasts, a few at a time, prawn side down, and deep-fry for 2–3 minutes, then turn and fry on the other side until golden.

5 Drain on kitchen paper and serve hot with sweet chilli sauce.

Nutritional information per portion: Energy 433Kcal/1806kJ; Protein 19.1g; Carbohydrate 27.7g, of which sugars 1.2g; Fat 27.6g, of which saturates 3.6g; Cholesterol 110mg; Calcium 271mg; Fibre 2.7g; Sodium 559mg.

Egg rolls

In some places, egg rolls are the same as spring rolls. These egg rolls, however, are wedges of a rolled Thai-flavoured omelette. They are frequently served as finger food.

SERVES 2

3 eggs, beaten
15ml/1 tbsp soy sauce
1 bunch garlic chives, thinly sliced
1–2 small fresh red or green chillies,
   seeded and finely chopped
small bunch fresh coriander
   (cilantro), chopped
pinch of granulated (white) sugar
salt and ground black pepper
15ml/1 tbsp groundnut (peanut) oil

FOR THE DIPPING SAUCE
60ml/4 tbsp light soy sauce
fresh lime juice, to taste

1 Make the dipping sauce. Pour the soy sauce into a bowl. Add a generous squeeze of lime juice. Taste and add more lime juice if needed.

2 Mix the eggs, soy sauce, chives, chillies and coriander. Add the sugar and season to taste. Heat the oil in a large frying pan, pour in the egg mixture and swirl the pan to make an omelette.

3 Cook for 1–2 minutes, until the omelette is just firm and the underside is golden. Slide it out on to a plate and roll up as though it were a pancake. Leave to cool completely.

4 When the omelette is cool, slice it diagonally in 1cm/$\frac{1}{2}$in pieces. Arrange the slices on a serving platter and serve with the bowl of dipping sauce.

Nutritional information per portion: Energy 189Kcal/780kJ; Protein 11.5g; Carbohydrate 1g, of which sugars 0.9g; Fat 15.3g, of which saturates 3.9g; Cholesterol 331mg; Calcium 76mg; Fibre 0.7g; Sodium 660mg.

Potato, shallot and garlic samosas with green peas

Most samosas are deep-fried. These are baked, making them a healthier option. They are also perfect for parties, since the pastries need no last-minute attention.

MAKES 25

1 large potato, about
    250g/9oz, diced
15ml/1 tbsp groundnut
    (peanut) oil
2 shallots, finely chopped
1 garlic clove, finely chopped
60ml/4 tbsp coconut milk
5ml/1 tsp Thai red or green
    curry paste

75g/3oz/³/4 cup peas
juice of ¹/2 lime
25 samosa wrappers or 10 x 5cm/
    4 x 2in strips of filo pastry
salt and ground black pepper
vegetable oil, for brushing

1 Preheat the oven to 220°C/425°F/Gas 7. Bring a small pan of water to the boil, add the diced potato, cover and cook for 10–15 minutes, until tender. Drain and set aside.

2 Meanwhile, heat the groundnut oil in a large frying pan and cook the shallots and garlic over a medium heat, stirring occasionally, for 4–5 minutes, until softened and golden.

3 Add the potato, coconut milk, red or green curry paste, peas and lime juice. Mash together coarsely with a wooden spoon. Season to taste with salt and pepper and cook over a low heat for 2–3 minutes, then remove the pan from the heat and set aside until the mixture has cooled a little.

4 Lay a samosa wrapper or filo strip flat on the work surface. Brush with a little oil, then place a generous teaspoonful of the mixture in the middle of one end. Turn one corner diagonally over the filling to meet the long edge.

5 Continue folding over the filling, keeping the triangular shape as you work down the strip. Brush with more oil if necessary and place on a baking sheet. Prepare the other samosas in the same way.

6 Bake for 15 minutes, or until the pastry is golden and crisp. Leave to cool slightly before serving.

Nutritional information per portion: Energy 360Kcal/1500kJ; Protein 13.7g; Carbohydrate 26.7g, of which sugars 9.8g; Fat 22.3g, of which saturates 2.9g; Cholesterol 98mg; Calcium 90mg; Fibre 0.3g; Sodium 711mg.

Firecrackers

It is easy to see how these pastry-wrapped prawn snacks acquired their name (krathak in Thai) – as well as resembling fireworks, their contents explode with flavour, making them irresistible.

MAKES 16

16 large, raw king prawns (jumbo
  shrimp), heads and shells removed but
  tails left on
5ml/1 tsp red curry paste
15ml/1 tbsp Thai fish sauce

16 small wonton wrappers, about
  8cm/3¼in square, thawed if frozen
16 fine egg noodles, soaked
vegetable oil, for deep-frying

1 Place the prawns on their sides and cut two slits through the underbelly of each, one about 1cm/½in from the head end and the other about 1cm/½in from the first cut, cutting across the prawn. This will prevent the prawns from curling when they are cooked.

2 Mix the curry paste with the fish sauce in a shallow dish. Add the prawns and turn them in the mixture until they are well coated. Cover and leave to marinate for 10 minutes.

3 Place a wonton wrapper on the work surface at an angle so that it forms a diamond shape, then fold the top corner over so that the point is in the centre. Place a prawn, slits facing down, on the wrapper, with the tail projecting from the folded end, then fold the bottom corner over the other end of the prawn.

4 Fold each side of the wrapper over in turn to make a tightly folded roll. Tie a noodle in a bow around the roll and set it aside. Repeat with the remaining prawns and wrappers.

5 Heat the oil in a large pan, deep-fryer or wok to 190°C/375°F or until a cube of bread, added to the oil, browns in 45 seconds. Fry the prawns, a few at a time, for 5–8 minutes, until golden brown and cooked through. Drain well on kitchen paper and keep hot while you cook the remaining batches.

Nutritional information per portion: Energy 110Kcal/457kJ; Protein 4.5g; Carbohydrate 7.6g, of which sugars 0g; Fat 6.8g, of which saturates 0.8g; Cholesterol 43mg; Calcium 20mg; Fibre 0.2g; Sodium 87mg.

Fish cakes with cucumber relish

These wonderful small fish cakes are a very familiar and popular appetizer in Thailand and increasingly throughout South-east Asia. They are usually served with Thai beer.

MAKES ABOUT 12

8 kaffir lime leaves

300g/11oz cod fillet, cut into chunks

30ml/2 tbsp red curry paste

1 egg

30ml/2 tbsp Thai fish sauce

5ml/1 tsp granulated (white) sugar

30ml/2 tbsp cornflour (cornstarch)

15ml/1 tbsp chopped fresh
    coriander (cilantro)

50g/2oz/$\frac{1}{2}$ cup green beans,
    thinly sliced

vegetable oil, for deep-frying

FOR THE CUCUMBER RELISH

60ml/4 tbsp coconut or rice vinegar

50g/2oz/$\frac{1}{4}$ cup granulated (white) sugar

60ml/4 tbsp water

1 head pickled garlic

1cm/$\frac{1}{2}$in piece fresh root ginger, peeled

1 cucumber, cut into thin batons

4 shallots, thinly sliced

1 Make the cucumber relish. Mix the coconut or rice vinegar, sugar and water in a pan. Heat gently, stirring, until the sugar has completely dissolved. Remove the pan from the heat and leave to cool.

2 Separate the pickled garlic into cloves. Chop the garlic cloves finely, along with the ginger, and place in a bowl. Add the cucumber batons and shallots, pour over the vinegar mixture and mix lightly. Cover and set aside.

3 Reserve five kaffir lime leaves for the garnish and thinly slice the remainder. Put the fish, curry paste and egg in a food processor and process to a smooth paste. Transfer this to a bowl and stir in the fish sauce, sugar, cornflour, sliced kaffir lime leaves, coriander and green beans. Mix well, then shape the mixture into about twelve 5mm/$\frac{1}{4}$in thick cakes, each one about 5cm/2in in diameter.

4 Heat the oil in a deep frying pan or wok to 190°C/375°F or until a cube of bread, added to the oil, browns in about 45 seconds. Fry the fish cakes, a few at a time, for about 4–5 minutes, until cooked and evenly brown.

5 Lift out the fish cakes and drain them on kitchen paper. Keep each batch hot while frying successive batches. Garnish with the reserved kaffir lime leaves and serve with the cucumber relish.

Nutritional information per portion: Energy 144Kcal/600kJ; Protein 5.4g; Carbohydrate 9.7g, of which sugars 5.1g; Fat 9.5g, of which saturates 1.4g; Cholesterol 30mg; Calcium 10mg; Fibre 0.2g; Sodium 25mg.

Corn fritters

Sometimes it is the simplest dishes that taste the best. These fritters, packed with crunchy corn, are very easy to prepare and understandably popular.

MAKES 12

3 corn cobs, total weight about 250g/9oz
1 garlic clove, crushed
small bunch fresh coriander
    (cilantro), chopped
1 small fresh red or green chilli, seeded
    and finely chopped
1 spring onion (scallion),
    finely chopped
15ml/1 tbsp soy sauce
75g/3oz/³⁄₄ cup rice flour or plain
    (all-purpose) flour
2 eggs, lightly beaten
60ml/4 tbsp water
vegetable oil, for shallow frying
salt and ground black pepper
sweet chilli sauce, to serve

1 Using a sharp knife, slice the kernels from the cobs and place them in a large bowl.

2 Add the garlic, coriander, chilli, spring onion, soy sauce, flour, beaten eggs, water and seasoning to taste and mix well. The mixture should be firm enough to hold its shape, but not stiff. Add more flour or water if necessary.

3 Heat the oil in a large frying pan. Add spoonfuls of the corn mixture, gently spreading each one out with the back of the spoon to make a roundish fritter. Cook for 1–2 minutes on each side, until golden.

4 Drain on kitchen paper and keep hot while frying more fritters in the same way. Serve hot with sweet chilli sauce.

Nutritional information per portion: Energy 76Kcal/315kJ; Protein 2.1g; Carbohydrate 7.6g, of which sugars 0.5g; Fat 4.1g, of which saturates 0.6g; Cholesterol 32mg; Calcium 12mg; Fibre 0.5g; Sodium 102mg.

Roasted coconut cashew nuts

Serve these hot and sweet cashew nuts in paper or cellophane cones at parties. Not only do they look enticing and taste terrific, but the cones help to keep clothes and hands clean.

SERVES 6–8

15ml/1 tbsp groundnut (peanut) oil
30ml/2 tbsp clear honey
250g/9oz/2 cups cashew nuts
115g/4oz/1⅓ cups desiccated (dry
   unsweetened shredded) coconut
2 small fresh red chillies, seeded and
   finely chopped
salt and ground black pepper

1 Heat the oil in a wok or large frying pan and then stir in the honey. After a few seconds add the nuts and coconut to the wok or frying pan and stir-fry until both are golden brown.

2 Add the chillies, with salt and pepper to taste. Toss until all the ingredients are well mixed. Serve the roasted cashew nuts warm or cooled in paper cones or small saucers.

Nutritional information per portion: Energy 436Kcal/1810kJ; Protein 9.7g; Carbohydrate 22.1g, of which sugars 16.6g; Fat 34.9g, of which saturates 14.8g; Cholesterol 0mg; Calcium 20mg; Fibre 4g; Sodium 128mg.

Thai tempeh cakes with sweet chilli dipping sauce

Made from soya beans, tempeh is similar to tofu but has a nuttier taste. Here, it is combined with a fragrant blend of lemon grass, coriander and ginger.

MAKES 8

1 lemon grass stalk, outer leaves
    removed and inside finely chopped
2 garlic cloves, chopped
2 spring onions (scallions),
    finely chopped
2 shallots, finely chopped
2 fresh red chillies, seeded and
    finely chopped
2.5cm/1in piece fresh root ginger,
    peeled and finely chopped
60ml/4 tbsp chopped fresh coriander
    (cilantro), plus extra to garnish
250g/9oz/2¼ cups tempeh, thawed if
    frozen, sliced
15ml/1 tbsp fresh lime juice
5ml/1 tsp granulated (white) sugar

45ml/3 tbsp plain (all-purpose) flour
1 large (US extra large) egg,
    lightly beaten
salt and ground black pepper
vegetable oil, for frying

FOR THE DIPPING SAUCE
45ml/3 tbsp mirin
45ml/3 tbsp white wine vinegar
2 spring onions (scallions), thinly sliced
15ml/1 tbsp granulated (white) sugar
2 fresh red chillies, seeded and
    finely chopped
30ml/2 tbsp chopped fresh
    coriander (cilantro)
large pinch of salt

1 Make the dipping sauce. Mix together the mirin, vinegar, spring onions, sugar, chillies, coriander and salt in a small bowl. Cover with clear film (plastic wrap) and set aside until ready to serve.

2 Place the lemon grass, garlic, spring onions, shallots, chillies, ginger and coriander in a blender or food processor, then process to a coarse paste. Add the tempeh, lime juice and sugar and process to combine. Add the flour and egg, and season. Process until the mixture forms a coarse, sticky paste.

3 Scrape the paste into a bowl. Take one-eighth of the mixture at a time and form it into rounds with your hands.

4 Heat a little oil in a large frying pan. Fry the tempeh cakes for 5–6 minutes, turning once, until golden. Drain on kitchen paper. Transfer to a platter, garnish with coriander and serve with the sauce.

Nutritional information per portion: Energy 148Kcal/611kJ; Protein 4.2g; Carbohydrate 5.4g, of which sugars 1g; Fat 12.3g, of which saturates 1.6g; Cholesterol 30mg; Calcium 174mg; Fibre 0.3g; Sodium 13mg.

Green curry puffs

Shrimp paste and green curry sauce, used judiciously, give these puffs their distinctive, spicy, savoury flavour, and the addition of chilli steps up the heat.

MAKES 24

24 small wonton wrappers, about 8cm/3¼in
　　square, thawed if frozen
15ml/1 tbsp cornflour (cornstarch), mixed to a
　　paste with 30ml/2 tbsp water
vegetable oil, for deep-frying

FOR THE FILLING
1 small potato, about 115g/4oz,
　　boiled and mashed
25g/1oz/3 tbsp cooked petits pois (baby peas)

25g/1oz/3 tbsp cooked corn
few sprigs fresh coriander
　　(cilantro), chopped
1 small fresh red chilli, seeded
　　and finely chopped
½ lemon grass stalk,
　　finely chopped
15ml/1 tbsp soy sauce
5ml/1 tsp shrimp paste or fish sauce
5ml/1 tsp Thai green curry paste

1 Combine the filling ingredients. Lay out one wonton wrapper and place a teaspoon of the filling in the centre.

2 Brush a little of the cornflour paste along two sides of the square. Fold the other two sides over to meet them, then press together to make a triangular pastry and seal in the filling. Make more pastries in the same way.

3 Heat the oil in a deep-fryer or wok to 190°C/375°F or until a cube of bread, added to the oil, browns in about 45 seconds. Add the pastries to the oil, a few at a time, and fry them for about 5 minutes, until golden brown.

4 Remove from the fryer or wok and drain on kitchen paper. If you intend serving the puffs hot, place them in a low oven while cooking successive batches. The puffs also taste good cold.

Nutritional information per portion: Energy 75Kcal/314kJ; Protein 1.1g; Carbohydrate 8.4g, of which sugars 0.6g; Fat 4.3g, of which saturates 0.6g; Cholesterol 0mg; Calcium 12mg; Fibre 0.4g; Sodium 70mg.

Fish and shellfish

Thailand has wonderful fish and shellfish dishes. The country has a long coastline, most of it on the fish-rich Gulf of Siam, and major rivers provide a wide variety of freshwater catches. Prawns and shrimp are popular both fresh and dried. The citrus flavours that are a feature of Thai curries work very well with fish and shellfish.

Sweet and sour fish

When fish such as red mullet or snapper is cooked in this way the skin becomes crisp, while the flesh inside remains moist and juicy. The sweet and sour sauce complements the fish beautifully.

SERVES 4–6

1 large or 2 medium fish, such as snapper
    or mullet, heads removed and rinsed
20ml/4 tsp cornflour (cornstarch)
120ml/4fl oz/½ cup vegetable oil
15ml/1 tbsp chopped garlic
15ml/1 tbsp chopped fresh root ginger
30ml/2 tbsp chopped shallots
225g/8oz cherry tomatoes
30ml/2 tbsp red wine vinegar
30ml/2 tbsp granulated (white) sugar
30ml/2 tbsp tomato ketchup
15ml/1 tbsp Thai fish sauce
45ml/3 tbsp water
salt and ground black pepper
coriander (cilantro) leaves and shredded
    spring onions (scallions), to garnish

1 Score the skin of the fish diagonally on both sides, then coat lightly with 15ml/1 tbsp of cornflour.

2 Heat the oil in a large frying pan or wok. Add the fish and cook over a medium heat for 6–7 minutes. Turn the fish over and cook for 6–7 minutes more, until crisp and brown.

3 Remove the fish and place on a large platter. Pour off all but 30ml/2 tbsp of the oil from the wok or pan and reheat the remainder.

4 Add the garlic, ginger and shallots to the pan and cook over a medium heat for 3–4 minutes, until golden. Add the cherry tomatoes and cook until they burst. Stir in the vinegar, sugar, tomato ketchup and fish sauce. Lower the heat and simmer for 2 minutes, then add more vinegar, sugar and/or fish sauce, to taste.

5 Mix the remaining cornflour with the water in a cup. Stir into the sauce. Heat, stirring, until it thickens. Pour over the fish, garnish and serve.

Nutritional information per portion: Energy 444Kcal/1856kJ; Protein 17.2g; Carbohydrate 39.7g, of which sugars 11.6g; Fat 25.2g, of which saturates 2.6g; Cholesterol 0mg; Calcium 78mg; Fibre 0.9g; Sodium 269mg.

Trout with tamarind and chilli sauce

Sometimes trout can taste rather bland, but this spicy sauce really gives it a zing. If you like your food very spicy, add an extra chilli.

SERVES 4

4 trout, cleaned
6 spring onions (scallions), sliced
60ml/4 tbsp soy sauce
15ml/1 tbsp vegetable oil
30ml/2 tbsp chopped fresh coriander
   (cilantro) and strips of fresh red chilli,
   to garnish

FOR THE SAUCE
50g/2oz tamarind pulp
105ml/7 tbsp boiling water
2 shallots, coarsely chopped
1 fresh red chilli, seeded and chopped
1cm/1/2in piece fresh root ginger,
   peeled and chopped
5ml/1 tsp soft light brown sugar
45ml/3 tbsp Thai fish sauce

1 Slash the trout diagonally four or five times on each side. Place in a shallow dish that is large enough to hold them all in a single layer.

2 Fill the cavities with spring onions and douse each fish with soy sauce. Turn over to coat both sides with the sauce. Sprinkle any remaining spring onions over the top.

3 Make the sauce. Put the tamarind pulp in a small bowl and pour on the boiling water. Mash well with a fork until softened.

4 Transfer the tamarind mixture to a food processor or blender, and add the shallots, fresh chilli, ginger, sugar and fish sauce. Process to a coarse pulp. Scrape into a bowl.

5 Heat the oil in a large frying pan or wok and cook the trout, one at a time if necessary, for 5 minutes on each side, until the skin is crisp and browned and the flesh cooked. Put on warmed plates and spoon over some of the sauce. Sprinkle with the coriander and chilli and serve with the remaining sauce.

Nutritional information per portion: Energy 193Kcal/813kJ; Protein 28.3g; Carbohydrate 2.8g, of which sugars 2.7g; Fat 7.7g, of which saturates 1.5g; Cholesterol 89mg; Calcium 38mg; Fibre 0.4g; Sodium 873mg.

Steamed fish with chilli sauce

Steaming is one of the best methods of cooking fish. By leaving the fish whole and on the bone, maximum flavour is retained and the flesh remains beautifully moist. The banana leaf is both authentic and attractive, but you can use baking parchment instead.

SERVES 4

1 large or 2 medium firm fish such as sea
    bass or grouper, scaled and cleaned
30ml/2 tbsp rice wine
3 fresh red chillies, seeded and
    thinly sliced
2 garlic cloves, finely chopped
2cm/3/4in piece fresh root ginger, peeled
    and finely shredded
2 lemon grass stalks, crushed and
    finely chopped
2 spring onions (scallions), chopped

30ml/2 tbsp Thai fish sauce
juice of 1 lime
1 fresh banana leaf

FOR THE CHILLI SAUCE
10 fresh red chillies, seeded
    and chopped
4 garlic cloves, chopped
60ml/4 tbsp Thai fish sauce
15ml/1 tbsp granulated (white) sugar
75ml/5 tbsp fresh lime juice

1 Thoroughly rinse the fish under cold running water. Pat it dry with kitchen paper. With a sharp knife, slash the skin of the fish a few times on both sides.

2 Mix together the rice wine, chillies, garlic, shredded ginger, lemon grass and spring onions in a non-metallic bowl. Add the fish sauce and lime juice and mix to a paste. Place the fish on the banana leaf and spread the spice paste evenly over it, rubbing it in well where the skin has been slashed.

3 Put a rack or a small upturned plate in the base of a wok. Pour in boiling water to a depth of 5cm/2in. Lift the banana leaf, together with the fish, and place it on the rack or plate. Cover with a lid and steam for 10–15 minutes, or until the fish is cooked.

4 Meanwhile, make the sauce. Place all the ingredients in a food processor and process until smooth. If the mixture seems to be too thick, add a little cold water. Scrape into a serving bowl.

5 Serve the fish hot, on the banana leaf if you like, with the sweet chilli sauce to spoon over the top.

Nutritional information per portion: Energy 123Kcal/519kJ; Protein 23.3g; Carbohydrate 0.8g, of which sugars 0.7g; Fat 3g, of which saturates 0.5g; Cholesterol 95mg; Calcium 158mg; Fibre 0.1g; Sodium 616mg.

Northern fish curry with shallots and lemon grass

This light curry is a fine example of a few carefully chosen ingredients combining to make a delicious dish. It is essential to use a stock that is well flavoured.

SERVES 4

450g/1lb salmon fillet
500ml/17fl oz/2¼ cups
   vegetable stock
4 shallots, finely chopped
2 garlic cloves, finely chopped
2.5cm/1in piece fresh galangal,
   finely chopped
1 lemon grass stalk, finely chopped
2.5ml/½ tsp dried chilli flakes
15ml/1 tbsp Thai fish sauce
5ml/1 tsp palm sugar (jaggery) or
   light muscovado (brown) sugar

1 Place the salmon in the freezer for 30–40 minutes to firm up the flesh slightly. Remove and discard the skin, then use a sharp knife to cut the fish into 2.5cm/1in cubes, removing any stray bones with your fingers or with tweezers as you do so.

2 Pour the stock into a large, heavy pan and bring it to the boil over a medium heat. Add the shallots, garlic, galangal, lemon grass, chilli flakes, fish sauce and sugar. Bring back to the boil, stir well, then reduce the heat and simmer gently for 15 minutes.

3 Add the fish, bring back to the boil, then turn off the heat. Leave the curry to stand for 10–15 minutes until the fish is cooked through, then serve.

Nutritional information per portion: Energy 212Kcal/882kJ; Protein 23.1g; Carbohydrate 1.7g, of which sugars 1.6g; Fat 12.5g, of which saturates 2.2g; Cholesterol 56mg; Calcium 28mg; Fibre 0.2g; Sodium 267mg.

Mussels and clams with lemon grass and coconut cream

Lemon grass has an incomparable aromatic flavour and is widely used with all kinds of seafood in Thailand as the tastes marry so perfectly.

SERVES 6

1.8kg/4lb fresh mussels
450g/1lb baby clams
120ml/4fl oz/¹/₂ cup dry white wine
1 bunch spring onions
    (scallions), chopped
2 lemon grass stalks, chopped
6 kaffir lime leaves, chopped
10ml/2 tsp Thai green curry paste
200ml/7fl oz/scant 1 cup
    coconut cream
30ml/2 tbsp chopped fresh
    coriander (cilantro)
salt and ground black pepper
garlic chives, to garnish

1 Pull off the beards, then scrub the mussels and clams. Discard any that are damaged or which are open and do not close when tapped sharply.

2 Put the wine in a large pan with the spring onions, lemon grass and lime leaves. Stir in the curry paste. Simmer until the wine has almost evaporated. Add the mussels and clams to the pan and increase the heat to high. Cover tightly and steam the shellfish for 5–6 minutes, until they open.

3 Transfer the shellfish to a heated serving bowl, cover and keep hot. Discard any that remain closed. Strain the cooking liquid into a clean pan through a sieve (strainer) lined with muslin (cheesecloth) and simmer briefly to reduce. Stir the coconut cream and coriander into the sauce and season. Heat through. Pour over the shellfish, garnish with garlic chives and serve immediately.

Nutritional information per portion: Energy 177Kcal/745kJ; Protein 21.8g; Carbohydrate 1.9g, of which sugars 1.2g; Fat 7.8g, of which saturates 5.3g; Cholesterol 58mg; Calcium 212mg; Fibre 0.3g; Sodium 594mg.

Curried seafood with coconut milk

This curry is based on a Thai classic. The lovely green colour is imparted by the finely chopped chilli and fresh herbs added during the last few moments of cooking.

SERVES 4

225g/8oz small ready-prepared squid
225g/8oz raw tiger prawns
    (jumbo shrimp)
400ml/14fl oz/1²/₃ cups coconut milk
2 kaffir lime leaves, finely shredded
30ml/2 tbsp Thai fish sauce
450g/1lb firm white fish fillets, skinned,
    boned and cut into chunks
2 fresh green chillies, seeded and
    finely chopped
30ml/2 tbsp torn fresh basil or coriander
    (cilantro) leaves
squeeze of fresh lime juice
cooked Thai jasmine rice,
    to serve

FOR THE CURRY PASTE

6 spring onions (scallions),
    coarsely chopped
4 fresh coriander (cilantro) stems,
    coarsely chopped, plus 45ml/3 tbsp
    chopped fresh coriander (cilantro)
4 kaffir lime leaves, shredded
8 fresh green chillies, seeded and
    coarsely chopped
1 lemon grass stalk,
    coarsely chopped
2.5cm/1in piece fresh root ginger, peeled
    and coarsely chopped
45ml/3 tbsp chopped fresh basil
15ml/1 tbsp vegetable oil

1 Make the curry paste. Put all the ingredients, except the oil, in a food processor and process to a paste. Alternatively, pound together in a mortar with a pestle. Stir in the oil.

2 Rinse the squid and pat dry with kitchen paper. Cut the bodies into rings and halve the tentacles, if they are large.

3 Heat a wok or heavy frying pan until hot, add the prawns and stir-fry, without any oil, for about 4 minutes, until they turn pink.

4 Remove the prawns from the wok or pan and leave to cool slightly, then peel, saving a few with shells on for the garnish. Make a slit along the back of each one and remove the black vein.

5 Pour the coconut milk into the wok or frying pan, then bring to the boil over a medium heat, stirring constantly.

6 Add 30ml/2 tbsp of the curry paste, the shredded lime leaves and fish sauce to the wok or pan and stir well to mix. Reduce the heat to low and simmer gently for about 10 minutes.

7 Add the squid, prawns and chunks of fish and cook for about 2 minutes, until the seafood is tender. Take care not to overcook the squid as it will become tough very quickly.

8 Just before serving, stir in the chillies and basil or coriander. Taste and adjust the flavour with a squeeze of lime juice. Garnish with prawns in their shells, and serve with Thai jasmine rice.

Nutritional information per portion: Energy 230Kcal/971kJ; Protein 39.9g; Carbohydrate 6.3g, of which sugars 5.6g; Fat 5.2g, of which saturates 0.9g; Cholesterol 288mg; Calcium 97mg; Fibre 0.2g; Sodium 614mg.

Crab and tofu stir-fry

For a year-round light meal, this speedy stir-fry is the ideal choice. As you need only a little crab meat – and you could use the canned variety – this is a very economical dish.

SERVES 2

250g/9oz silken tofu
60ml/4 tbsp vegetable oil
2 garlic cloves, finely chopped
115g/4oz white crab meat
130g/4½oz/generous 1 cup baby corn,
    halved lengthways
2 spring onions (scallions), chopped
1 fresh red chilli, seeded and
    finely chopped
30ml/2 tbsp soy sauce
15ml/1 tbsp Thai fish sauce
5ml/1 tsp palm sugar (jaggery) or
    light muscovado (brown) sugar
juice of 1 lime
small bunch fresh coriander (cilantro),
    chopped, to garnish

1 Using a sharp knife, cut the silken tofu into 1cm/½in cubes.

2 Heat the oil in a wok or large, heavy frying pan. Add the tofu cubes and stir-fry until golden all over, taking care not to break them up. Remove the tofu with a slotted spoon and set aside.

3 Add the garlic to the wok and stir-fry until golden. Add the crab meat, tofu, corn, spring onions, chilli, soy sauce, fish sauce and sugar.

4 Cook, stirring constantly, until the vegetables are just tender. Stir in the lime juice, transfer to warmed bowls, sprinkle with coriander and serve.

Nutritional information per portion: Energy 370Kcal/1532kJ; Protein 23.3g; Carbohydrate 6.2g, of which sugars 5.1g; Fat 28.1g, of which saturates 3.3g; Cholesterol 41mg; Calcium 720mg; Fibre 1.2g; Sodium 2487mg.

Stir-fried prawns with tamarind

The sour, tangy flavour that is characteristic of many Thai dishes comes from tamarind. You can make your own from fresh tamarind pods but it is much easier to use a block of tamarind paste.

SERVES 4–6

6 dried red chillies
30ml/2 tbsp vegetable oil
30ml/2 tbsp chopped onion
30ml/2 tbsp palm sugar (jaggery) or
 light muscovado (brown) sugar
30ml/2 tbsp chicken stock or water
15ml/1 tbsp Thai fish sauce
90ml/6 tbsp tamarind juice, made
 by mixing tamarind paste with
 warm water
450g/1lb raw prawns
 (shrimp), peeled
15ml/1 tbsp fried chopped garlic
30ml/2 tbsp fried sliced shallots
2 spring onions (scallions), chopped,
 to garnish

1 Heat a wok or large frying pan, but do not add any oil at this stage. Add the dried chillies and dry-fry them by pressing them against the surface of the wok with a spatula, turning occasionally. Do not let them burn. Set aside to cool slightly.

2 Add the oil to the wok or pan and reheat. Add the chopped onion and cook over a medium heat, stirring occasionally, for 2–3 minutes, until softened and golden brown.

3 Add the sugar, stock or water, fish sauce, chillies and tamarind juice, stirring constantly until the sugar has dissolved. Bring to the boil, then lower the heat slightly.

4 Add the prawns, garlic and shallots to the other ingredients in the wok or pan. Toss over the heat for 3–4 minutes, until the prawns are cooked. Transfer to individual bowls, garnish with the spring onions and serve immediately.

Nutritional information per portion: Energy 185Kcal/776kJ; Protein 20.6g; Carbohydrate 9.7g, of which sugars 8.4g; Fat 7.4g, of which saturates 0.9g; Cholesterol 219mg; Calcium 102mg; Fibre 0.7g; Sodium 393mg.

Satay prawns

This delicious dish is inspired by the classic Indonesian satay. The combination of crunchy peanut butter, aromatic spices, sweet coconut milk and zesty lemon juice in the spicy dip is perfect and is guaranteed to have guests coming back for more.

SERVES 4–6

450g/1lb king prawns (jumbo shrimp)
25ml/1¹⁄₂ tbsp vegetable oil

FOR THE PEANUT SAUCE
25ml/1¹⁄₂ tbsp vegetable oil
15ml/1 tbsp chopped garlic
1 small onion, chopped
3–4 fresh red chillies, seeded
    and chopped
3 kaffir lime leaves, torn
1 lemon grass stalk, bruised
    and chopped
5ml/1 tsp medium curry paste
250ml/8fl oz/1 cup coconut milk
1cm/¹⁄₂in piece cinnamon stick
75g/3oz/¹⁄₃ cup crunchy
    peanut butter

45ml/3 tbsp tamarind juice, made
    by mixing tamarind paste with
    warm water
30ml/2 tbsp Thai fish sauce
30ml/2 tbsp palm sugar (jaggery) or
    light muscovado (brown) sugar
juice of ¹⁄₂ lemon

FOR THE GARNISH
¹⁄₂ bunch fresh coriander
    (cilantro) leaves (optional)
4 fresh red chillies, finely sliced (optional)
spring onions (scallions),
    cut diagonally

1 Remove the heads from the prawns and peel, leaving the tail ends intact. Slit each prawn along the back with a small, sharp knife and remove the black vein. Rinse the prawns under cold running water, pat completely dry on kitchen paper and set aside.

2 Make the peanut sauce. Heat half the oil in a wok or large, heavy frying pan. Add the garlic and onion and cook over a medium heat, stirring occasionally, for 3–4 minutes, until the mixture has softened but not browned.

3 Add the chillies, kaffir lime leaves, lemon grass and curry paste. Stir well and cook for a further 2–3 minutes, then stir in the coconut milk, cinnamon stick, peanut butter, tamarind juice, fish sauce, sugar and lemon juice. Cook, stirring constantly, until well blended.

4 Bring to the boil, then reduce the heat to low and simmer for 15–20 minutes, until the sauce thickens. Stir occasionally to prevent the sauce from sticking.

5 Thread the prawns on to skewers and brush with a little oil. Cook under a preheated grill (broiler) for 2 minutes on each side until they turn pink and are firm to the touch. Alternatively, pan-fry the prawns, then thread on to skewers.

6 Remove the cinnamon stick from the sauce and discard. Arrange the skewered prawns on a warmed platter, garnish with spring onions and coriander leaves and sliced red chillies, if using, and serve with the sauce.

Nutritional information per portion: Energy 321Kcal/1340kJ; Protein 24.6g; Carbohydrate 13.5g, of which sugars 11.9g; Fat 19.1g, of which saturates 3.6g; Cholesterol 219mg; Calcium 122mg; Fibre 1.2g; Sodium 794mg.

Stir-fried prawns with noodles

One of the most appealing aspects of Thai food is its appearance. Ingredients are carefully chosen so that each dish is balanced in terms of colour, texture and flavour.

SERVES 4

150g/5oz large prawns (shrimp)
130g/4¹/₂oz rice noodles
30ml/2 tbsp groundnut (peanut) oil
1 large garlic clove, crushed
15g/¹/₂oz dried shrimp
75g/3oz mooli (daikon), grated
15ml/1 tbsp Thai fish sauce
30ml/2 tbsp soy sauce
30ml/2 tbsp palm sugar (jaggery) or light muscovado (brown) sugar
30ml/2 tbsp fresh lime juice
90g/3¹/₂oz/1³/₄ cups beansprouts
40g/1¹/₂oz/¹/₃ cup peanuts, chopped
15ml/1 tbsp sesame oil
chopped coriander (cilantro), 5ml/1 tsp dried chilli flakes and 2 shallots, finely chopped, to garnish

1 Peel and devein the prawns. Soak the noodles in a bowl of boiling water for 5 minutes, or according to the packet instructions. Heat the oil in a wok or large frying pan. Add the garlic, and stir-fry over a medium heat for 2–3 minutes, until golden brown.

2 Add the prawns, dried shrimp and grated mooli to the pan and stir-fry for a further 2 minutes. Stir in the fish sauce, soy sauce, sugar and lime juice.

3 Drain the noodles thoroughly, then snip them into smaller lengths with scissors. Add to the wok or pan with the beansprouts, peanuts and sesame oil. Toss to mix, then stir-fry for 2 minutes. Serve immediately, garnished with the coriander, chilli flakes and shallots.

Nutritional information per portion: Energy 312Kcal/1299kJ; Protein 11.8g; Carbohydrate 35.8g, of which sugars 8.2g; Fat 13.3g, of which saturates 2.4g; Cholesterol 73mg; Calcium 52mg; Fibre 1.1g; Sodium 524mg.

Stir-fried squid with ginger

The abundance of fish around the Gulf of Thailand sustains thriving markets where delicious, freshly-caught seafood is cooked and served. This recipe is popular among street traders.

SERVES 2

4 ready-prepared baby squid, total weight about 250g/9oz
15ml/1 tbsp vegetable oil
2 garlic cloves, finely chopped
30ml/2 tbsp soy sauce
2.5cm/1in piece fresh root ginger, peeled and finely chopped
juice of 1/2 lemon
5ml/1 tsp granulated (white) sugar
2 spring onions (scallions), chopped

1 Rinse the squid well and pat dry with kitchen paper. Cut the bodies into rings and halve the tentacles, if they are large.

2 Heat the vegetable oil in a wok or frying pan and gently cook the garlic until it is golden brown, but be careful not to let it burn or it will taste bitter.

3 Add the squid to the pan and stir-fry for 30 seconds over a high heat.

4 Add the soy sauce, ginger, lemon juice, sugar and spring onions. Stir-fry for a further 30 seconds, then serve.

COOK'S TIP
Squid has an undeserved reputation for being rubbery in texture. This is always a result of overcooking it.

Nutritional information per portion: Energy 168Kcal/704kJ; Protein 19.9g; Carbohydrate 5.1g, of which sugars 3.5g; Fat 7.7g, of which saturates 1.2g; Cholesterol 281mg; Calcium 24mg; Fibre 0.2g; Sodium 1207mg.

Pan-steamed mussels with Thai herbs

Like so many Thai dishes, this is very easy to prepare. The lemon grass and kaffir lime leaves add a refreshing tang to the mussels.

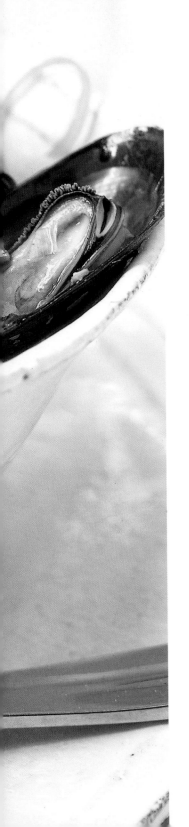

SERVES 4–6

1kg/2¼lb fresh mussels
2 lemon grass stalks, finely chopped
4 shallots, chopped
4 kaffir lime leaves, coarsely torn
2 fresh red chillies, sliced

15ml/1 tbsp Thai fish sauce
30ml/2 tbsp fresh lime juice
thinly sliced spring onions (scallions)
    and coriander (cilantro) leaves,
    to garnish

1 Clean the mussels by pulling off the beards, scrubbing the shells well and removing any barnacles. Discard any mussels that are broken or which are open and do not close when tapped sharply.

2 Place the mussels in a large, heavy pan and add the lemon grass, shallots, kaffir lime leaves, chillies, fish sauce and lime juice. Mix well. Cover the pan tightly and steam the mussels over a high heat, shaking the pan occasionally, for 5–7 minutes, until the shells have opened.

3 Using a slotted spoon, transfer the cooked mussels to a warmed serving dish or individual bowls. Discard any mussels that have failed to open.

4 Garnish the mussels with the thinly sliced spring onions and coriander leaves. Serve immediately.

Nutritional information per portion: Energy 66Kcal/282kJ; Protein 13.1g; Carbohydrate 0.2g, of which sugars 0.2g; Fat 1.5g, of which saturates 0.3g; Cholesterol 30mg; Calcium 148mg; Fibre 0g; Sodium 336mg.

Poultry and meat

The majority of meat dishes in Thailand

are curries, with chillies, garlic, ginger or

galangal as the predominant flavourings,

often with lemon grass and coriander. One

of the notable features of most Thai meat

dishes is the speed with which they are

prepared. Of course, short cooking times

depend on tender, good quality meat.

Southern chicken curry

This is a mild coconut curry flavoured with turmeric, coriander and cumin seeds that demonstrates the influence of Malaysian cooking on Thai cuisine.

SERVES 4

60ml/4 tbsp vegetable oil

1 large garlic clove, crushed

1 chicken, weighing about 1.5kg/
   3–3¹/₂lb, chopped into
   12 large pieces

400ml/14fl oz/1²/₃ cups
   coconut cream

250ml/8fl oz/1 cup chicken stock

30ml/2 tbsp Thai fish sauce

30ml/2 tbsp sugar

juice of 2 limes

FOR THE CURRY PASTE

5ml/1 tsp dried chilli flakes

2.5ml/¹/₂ tsp salt

5cm/2in piece fresh turmeric or 5ml/1 tsp
   ground turmeric

2.5ml/¹/₂ tsp coriander seeds

2.5ml/¹/₂ tsp cumin seeds

5ml/1 tsp dried shrimp paste

TO GARNISH

2 small fresh red chillies, seeded
   and chopped

1 bunch spring onions (scallions), sliced

1 For the curry paste, put all the ingredients in a mortar, food processor or spice grinder and pound, process or grind to a smooth paste.

2 Heat the oil in a wok or large frying pan and cook the garlic until golden. Add the chicken and cook until golden on all sides. Remove the chicken and set aside.

3 Reheat the oil and add the curry paste and then half the coconut cream. Cook, stirring, for a few minutes until fragrant.

4 Return the chicken to the wok or pan, add the stock, mixing well, then add the remaining coconut cream, the fish sauce, sugar and lime juice. Stir well and bring to the boil, then lower the heat and simmer for 15 minutes.

5 Turn the curry into four warm serving bowls and sprinkle with the chopped fresh chillies and spring onions to garnish. Serve immediately.

Nutritional information per portion: Energy 612Kcal/2541kJ; Protein 38.5g; Carbohydrate 9g, of which sugars 8.9g; Fat 47.1g, of which saturates 26.4g; Cholesterol 139mg; Calcium 22mg; Fibre 0g; Sodium 447mg.

Red chicken curry with bamboo shoots

Bamboo shoots have a lovely crunchy texture and are great in currys. Fresh bamboo is not readily available in the West. When buying the canned variety, choose whole bamboo shoots, which are crisper and of better quality than sliced shoots.

SERVES 4–6

1 litre/1¾ pints/4 cups coconut milk
450g/1lb skinless, boneless chicken
    breast portions, diced
30ml/2 tbsp Thai fish sauce
15ml/1 tbsp granulated (white) sugar
1–2 drained canned bamboo shoots,
    about 225g/8oz, rinsed and sliced
5 kaffir lime leaves, torn
salt and ground black pepper
chopped fresh red chillies and kaffir lime
    leaves, to garnish

FOR THE RED CURRY PASTE
5ml/1 tsp coriander seeds
2.5ml/½ tsp cumin seeds

12–15 fresh red chillies, seeded
    and coarsely chopped
4 shallots, thinly sliced
2 garlic cloves, chopped
15ml/1 tbsp chopped
    fresh galangal
2 lemon grass stalks, chopped
3 kaffir lime leaves, chopped
4 fresh coriander (cilantro) roots
10 black peppercorns
good pinch ground cinnamon
5ml/1 tsp ground turmeric
2.5ml/½ tsp shrimp paste
5ml/1 tsp salt
30ml/2 tbsp vegetable oil

1 Make the curry paste. Dry-fry the coriander seeds and cumin seeds for 1–2 minutes, then put in a mortar or food processor with the remaining ingredients except the oil. Pound or process to a paste.

2 Add the vegetable oil, a little at a time, mixing or processing well after each addition. Transfer to a screw-top jar, put on the lid and keep in the refrigerator until ready to use.

3 Pour half of the coconut milk into a large, heavy pan. Bring to the boil over a medium heat, stirring constantly until the coconut milk has separated.

4 Stir in 30ml/2 tbsp of the red curry paste and cook the mixture, stirring constantly, for 2–3 minutes, until the curry paste is thoroughly incorporated. The remaining red curry paste can be kept in the closed jar in the refrigerator for up to 3 months.

5 Add the chicken, fish sauce and sugar to the pan. Stir well, then lower the heat and cook gently for 5–6 minutes, stirring, until the chicken changes colour and is cooked. Take care that the curry does not stick to the pan.

6 Pour the remaining coconut milk into the pan, then add the sliced bamboo shoots and torn lime leaves. Bring back to the boil over a medium heat, stirring constantly to prevent the mixture from sticking to the pan, then taste and add salt and pepper if necessary.

7 To serve, spoon the curry into a warmed serving dish and garnish with the chopped chillies and lime leaves.

Nutritional information per portion: Energy 255Kcal/1077kJ; Protein 29.5g; Carbohydrate 18g, of which sugars 16.9g; Fat 7.8g, of which saturates 1.5g; Cholesterol 79mg; Calcium 92mg; Fibre 0.9g; Sodium 1104mg.

Green chicken curry

Use one or two fresh green chillies in this dish, depending on how hot you like your curry.
The mild aromatic flavour of the rice is a good foil for the spicy chicken.

SERVES 3–4

4 spring onions (scallions), trimmed and
    coarsely chopped
1–2 fresh green chillies, seeded and
    coarsely chopped
2cm/$\frac{3}{4}$in piece fresh root ginger, peeled
2 garlic cloves
5ml/1 tsp Thai fish sauce
large bunch fresh coriander (cilantro)
small handful fresh parsley
30–45ml/2–3 tbsp water
30ml/2 tbsp sunflower oil

4 skinless, boneless chicken breast
    portions, diced
1 green (bell) pepper, seeded and
    thinly sliced
600ml/1 pint/2$\frac{1}{2}$ cups coconut milk or
    75g/3oz piece of creamed coconut
    dissolved in 400ml/14fl oz/
    1$\frac{2}{3}$ cups boiling water
salt and ground black pepper
hot coconut rice, to serve

1 Put the spring onions, green chillies, ginger, garlic, fish sauce, coriander and parsley in a food processor or blender. Pour in 30ml/2 tbsp of the water and process to a smooth paste, adding a further 15ml/1 tbsp water if required.

2 Heat half the oil in a large frying pan. Cook the diced chicken until evenly browned. Remove from the pan and transfer to a plate.

3 Heat the remaining oil in the frying pan. Add the green pepper and stir-fry for 3–4 minutes, then add the chilli and ginger paste. Stir-fry for 3–4 minutes, until the mixture becomes fairly thick.

4 Return the chicken to the pan and add the coconut liquid. Season with salt and pepper and bring to the boil, then reduce the heat, half cover the pan with the lid and simmer for 8–10 minutes.

5 When the chicken is cooked, transfer it, with the green pepper, to a plate. Boil the cooking liquid remaining in the pan for 10–12 minutes, until it is well reduced and fairly thick.

6 Return the chicken and pepper to the green curry sauce, stir well and cook gently for 2–3 minutes to heat through. Spoon the curry over the coconut rice and serve immediately.

Nutritional information per portion: Energy 334Kcal/1413kJ; Protein 49.4g; Carbohydrate 11.9g, of which sugars 11.7g; Fat 10.4g, of which saturates 2g; Cholesterol 140mg; Calcium 78mg; Fibre 1.1g; Sodium 462mg.

Chicken and lemon grass curry

This fragrant and truly delicious curry is exceptionally easy and takes less than 20 minutes to prepare and cook – making it a perfect mid-week meal.

SERVES 4

45ml/3 tbsp vegetable oil

2 garlic cloves, crushed

500g/1¼lb skinless, boneless chicken
   thighs, chopped into small pieces

45ml/3 tbsp Thai fish sauce

120ml/4fl oz/½ cup chicken stock

5ml/1 tsp granulated (white) sugar

1 lemon grass stalk, chopped into
   4 sticks and lightly crushed

5 kaffir lime leaves, rolled into cylinders
   and thinly sliced, plus extra to garnish

chopped roasted peanuts and chopped
   fresh coriander (cilantro), to garnish

FOR THE CURRY PASTE

1 lemon grass stalk, chopped

2.5cm/1in piece galangal, peeled
   and chopped

2 kaffir lime leaves, chopped

3 shallots, coarsely chopped

6 coriander (cilantro) roots, chopped

2 garlic cloves

2 green chillies, seeded and chopped

5ml/1 tsp shrimp paste

5ml/1 tsp ground turmeric

1 Make the curry paste. Place all the ingredients in a large mortar or food processor and pound with a pestle or process to a smooth paste.

2 Heat the vegetable oil in a wok or large, heavy frying pan, add the garlic and cook over a low heat, stirring frequently, until golden brown. Be careful not to let the garlic burn or it will taste bitter. Add the curry paste and stir-fry with the garlic for about 30 seconds more.

3 Add the chicken and stir until well coated with the curry paste.

4 Stir in the Thai fish sauce and chicken stock, with the sugar, and cook, stirring constantly, for 2 minutes more.

5 Add the lemon grass and lime leaves, reduce the heat and simmer for 10 minutes. If the mixture begins to dry out, add a little more stock or water.

6 Remove the lemon grass, if you like. Spoon the curry into four dishes, garnish with the lime leaves, peanuts and coriander and serve immediately.

Nutritional information per portion: Energy 212Kcal/890kJ; Protein 30.1g; Carbohydrate 1.4g, of which sugars 1.3g; Fat 9.6g, of which saturates 1.4g; Cholesterol 88mg; Calcium 8mg; Fibre 0g; Sodium 342mg.

Yellow chicken curry

The pairing of slightly sweet coconut milk and fruit with savoury chicken and spices is at once a comforting, refreshing and exotic combination.

SERVES 4

300ml/½ pint/1¼ cups chicken stock
30ml/2 tbsp thick tamarind juice, made by
    mixing tamarind paste with warm water
15ml/1 tbsp granulated (white) sugar
200ml/7fl oz/scant 1 cup coconut milk
1 green papaya, peeled, seeded and sliced
250g/9oz skinless, boneless chicken
    breast portions, diced
juice of 1 lime
lime slices, to garnish

FOR THE CURRY PASTE
1 red chilli, seeded and coarsely chopped
4 garlic cloves, coarsely chopped
3 shallots, coarsely chopped
2 lemon grass stalks, sliced
5cm/2in piece fresh turmeric, coarsely
    chopped, or 5ml/1 tsp ground turmeric
5ml/1 tsp shrimp paste
5ml/1 tsp salt

1 First make the curry paste. Put the red chilli, garlic, shallots, lemon grass and turmeric in a mortar or food processor. Add the shrimp paste and salt. Pound or process to a paste, adding a little water if necessary.

2 Pour the stock into a wok or medium pan and bring it to the boil. Stir in the curry paste.

3 Bring back to the boil and add the tamarind juice, sugar, coconut milk, papaya and chicken to the pan and cook over a medium to high heat for about 15 minutes, stirring frequently, until the chicken is cooked.

4 Stir in the lime juice, transfer to a warm dish and serve immediately, garnished with lime slices.

Nutritional information per portion: Energy 125Kcal/533kJ; Protein 15.7g; Carbohydrate 14.2g, of which sugars 14.1g; Fat 1.1g, of which saturates 0.3g; Cholesterol 44mg; Calcium 41mg; Fibre 1.9g; Sodium 956mg.

Cashew chicken

Although it is not native to South-east Asia, the cashew tree is highly prized in Thailand and the classic partnership of these slightly sweet nuts with chicken is immensely popular.

SERVES 4–6

450g/1lb boneless chicken
   breast portions
30ml/2 tbsp vegetable oil
1 red (bell) pepper, diced
2 garlic cloves, thinly sliced
4 dried red chillies, chopped
30ml/2 tbsp oyster sauce
15ml/1 tbsp soy sauce

pinch of granulated (white) sugar
1 bunch spring onions (scallions), cut into
   5cm/2in lengths
175g/6oz/1½ cups cashew nuts, roasted
coriander (cilantro) leaves,
   to garnish

1 Remove and discard the skin from the chicken breasts and trim off any excess fat. With a sharp knife, cut the chicken into bitesize pieces and set aside.

2 Preheat a wok and then heat the oil. The best way to do this is to drizzle a "necklace" of oil around the inner rim of the wok, so that it drops down to coat the entire inner surface. Make sure the coating is even by swirling the wok.

3 Add the garlic and dried chillies to the wok and stir-fry over a medium heat until golden. Do not let the garlic burn, otherwise it will taste bitter.

4 Add the chicken to the wok and stir-fry until it is cooked through, then add the red pepper. If the mixture is very dry, add a little water.

5 Stir in the oyster sauce, soy sauce and sugar. Add the spring onions and cashew nuts. Stir-fry for 1–2 minutes more, until heated through. Spoon into a warm dish and serve immediately, garnished with the coriander leaves.

Nutritional information per portion: Energy 458Kcal/1909kJ; Protein 37.1g; Carbohydrate 12.2g, of which sugars 6.2g; Fat 29.3g, of which saturates 5.5g; Cholesterol 79mg; Calcium 35mg; Fibre 2.5g; Sodium 554mg.

Fragrant grilled chicken

If you have time, prepare the chicken in advance and leave it to marinate in the refrigerator for several hours – or even overnight – until ready to cook.

SERVES 4

450g/1lb boneless chicken breast
    portions, with the skin on
30ml/2 tbsp sesame oil
2 garlic cloves, crushed
2 coriander (cilantro) roots,
    finely chopped
2 small fresh red chillies, seeded
    and finely chopped
30ml/2 tbsp Thai fish sauce
5ml/1 tsp sugar
lime wedges, to garnish
cooked rice, to serve

FOR THE SAUCE
90ml/6 tbsp rice vinegar
60ml/4 tbsp sugar
2.5ml/$\frac{1}{2}$ tsp salt
2 garlic cloves, crushed
1 small fresh red chilli, seeded and
    finely chopped
115g/4oz/4 cups fresh coriander
    (cilantro), finely chopped

1 Lay the chicken breast portions between two sheets of clear film (plastic wrap), baking parchment or foil and beat with the side of a rolling pin or the flat side of a meat tenderizer until the meat is about half its original thickness. Place in a large, shallow dish or bowl.

2 Mix together the sesame oil, garlic, coriander roots, red chillies, fish sauce and sugar in a jug (pitcher), stirring until the sugar has dissolved. Pour the mixture over the chicken and turn to coat. Cover with clear film and set aside to marinate in a cool place for at least 20 minutes. Meanwhile, make the sauce.

3 Heat the vinegar in a small pan, add the sugar and stir until dissolved. Add the salt and stir over a medium heat until the mixture begins to thicken. Add the remaining sauce ingredients, stir well, then spoon the sauce into a serving bowl.

4 Preheat the grill (broiler) and cook the chicken for 5 minutes. Turn and baste with the marinade, then cook for 5 minutes more, or until cooked through and golden. Place on a warmed serving dish, garnish with lime wedges and serve with rice and the sauce.

Nutritional information per portion: Energy 243Kcal/1022kJ; Protein 28g; Carbohydrate 17.7g, of which sugars 17.6g; Fat 7.1g, of which saturates 1.2g; Cholesterol 79mg; Calcium 73mg; Fibre 1.5g; Sodium 502mg.

Roast lime chicken with sweet potatoes

In Thailand, this chicken would be spit-roasted, as ovens are seldom used. However, it works very well as a conventional roast. The sweet potatoes are an inspired addition.

SERVES 4

4 garlic cloves, 2 finely chopped
    and 2 bruised but left whole
small bunch coriander (cilantro),
    with roots, coarsely chopped
5ml/1 tsp ground turmeric
5cm/2in piece fresh turmeric
1 roasting chicken, about 1.5kg/3¼lb

1 lime, cut in half
4 medium/large sweet potatoes, peeled
    and cut into thick wedges
300ml/½ pint/1¼ cups chicken
    or vegetable stock
30ml/2 tbsp soy sauce
salt and ground black pepper

1 Preheat the oven to 190°C/375°F/Gas 5. Calculate the cooking time for the chicken, allowing 20 minutes per 500g/1¼lb, plus 20 minutes. Using a mortar and pestle or food processor, grind the chopped garlic, coriander, 10ml/2 tsp salt and turmeric to a paste.

2 Place the chicken in a roasting pan and smear it with the paste. Squeeze the lime juice over and place the lime halves and the bruised whole garlic cloves in the cavity. Cover with foil and roast in the oven.

3 Meanwhile, bring a pan of water to the boil. Par-boil the sweet potatoes for 10–15 minutes, until just tender. Drain and place them around the chicken in the roasting pan. Baste with the cooking juices and sprinkle with salt and pepper. Replace the foil and return the chicken to the oven. About 20 minutes before the end of cooking, remove the foil and baste the chicken. Turn the sweet potatoes over.

4 Check that the chicken is cooked. Tilt it so that all the juices collected in the cavity drain into the pan, then place the bird on a carving board. Cover with tented foil and leave to rest before carving. Transfer the sweet potatoes to a serving dish and keep hot while you make the gravy.

5 Pour away the oil from the roasting pan but keep the juices. Place the pan on top of the stove and heat until the juices are bubbling. Pour in the stock. Bring to the boil, stirring constantly and scraping the base to incorporate the residue. Stir in the soy sauce and check the seasoning before straining the gravy into a jug (pitcher). Serve with the carved meat and the sweet potatoes.

Nutritional information per portion: Energy 529Kcal/2201kJ; Protein 47.3g; Carbohydrate 8.7g, of which sugars 2.7g; Fat 34g, of which saturates 9.4g; Cholesterol 248mg; Calcium 26mg; Fibre 0.9g; Sodium 840mg.

Chinese duck curry

A richly spiced curry that illustrates the powerful Chinese influence on Thai cuisine. The duck is best marinated overnight in the refrigerator.

SERVES 4

4 duck breast portions, skin and bones
   removed, cut into bitesize pieces
30ml/2 tbsp five-spice powder
30ml/2 tbsp sesame oil
grated rind and juice of 1 orange
1 medium butternut squash, peeled
   and cubed
10ml/2 tsp Thai red curry paste
30ml/2 tbsp Thai fish sauce
15ml/1 tbsp palm sugar (jaggery) or
   light muscovado (brown) sugar
300ml/½ pint/1¼ cups coconut milk
2 fresh red chillies, seeded
4 kaffir lime leaves, torn
small bunch coriander (cilantro),
   chopped, to garnish

1 Place the duck in a bowl with the five-spice powder, sesame oil and orange rind and juice. Stir well to coat the duck with marinade. Cover with clear film (plastic wrap) and set aside for at least 15 minutes.

2 Meanwhile, bring a pan of water to the boil. Add the squash and cook for 10–15 minutes, until just tender. Drain and set aside.

3 Pour the marinade from the duck into a wok and heat until boiling.

4 Stir in the curry paste and cook for 2–3 minutes. Add the duck and cook for 3–4 minutes, stirring constantly, until browned on all sides.

5 Add the fish sauce and sugar and cook for 2 minutes more. Stir in the coconut milk until the mixture is smooth, then add the squash, with the chillies and lime leaves.

6 Simmer gently, stirring often, for 5 minutes, then spoon into a dish, sprinkle with coriander and serve.

Nutritional information per portion: Energy 297Kcal/1245kJ; Protein 30.3g; Carbohydrate 9.4g, of which sugars 9.1g; Fat 15.7g, of which saturates 4.1g; Cholesterol 165mg; Calcium 67mg; Fibre 0.6g; Sodium 275mg.

Duck and sesame stir-fry

This recipe comes from northern Thailand and is intended for game birds, as farmed duck would have too much fat. Use wild duck if you can get it, or even partridge, pheasant or pigeon.

SERVES 4

250g/9oz boneless wild duck meat
15ml/1 tbsp sesame oil
15ml/1 tbsp vegetable oil
4 garlic cloves, finely sliced
2.5ml/¹⁄₂ tsp dried chilli flakes
15ml/1 tbsp Thai fish sauce
15ml/1 tbsp light soy sauce
120ml/4fl oz/¹⁄₂ cup water
1 head broccoli, cut into small florets
coriander (cilantro) and 15ml/1 tbsp
   toasted sesame seeds, to garnish

1 Cut the duck meat into bitesize pieces. Heat the oils in a wok or large, heavy frying pan and stir-fry the garlic over a medium heat until it is golden brown – do not let it burn. Add the duck to the pan and stir-fry for a further 2 minutes, until the meat begins to brown.

2 Stir in the chilli flakes, fish sauce, soy sauce and water. Add the broccoli and continue to stir-fry for about 2 minutes, until the duck is just cooked through.

3 Serve on warmed plates, garnished with coriander and sesame seeds.

Nutritional information per portion: Energy 152Kcal/634kJ; Protein 14.4g; Carbohydrate 1.3g, of which sugars 1.1g; Fat 10g, of which saturates 2.1g; Cholesterol 69mg; Calcium 33mg; Fibre 1.1g; Sodium 517mg.

Jungle curry of guinea fowl

A traditional wild food country curry from the north-central region of Thailand, this dish can be made using any game, fish or chicken. Guinea fowl is not typical of Thai cuisine, but is widely available in the West and adds a delicious flavour to this dish.

SERVES 4

1 guinea fowl or similar game bird

15ml/1 tbsp vegetable oil

10ml/2 tsp green curry paste

15ml/1 tbsp Thai fish sauce

2.5cm/1in piece fresh galangal, peeled
   and finely chopped

15ml/1 tbsp fresh green peppercorns

3 kaffir lime leaves, torn

15ml/1 tbsp whisky,
   preferably Mekhong

300ml/1/2 pint/11/4 cups chicken stock

50g/2oz snake beans or yard-long
   beans, cut into 2.5cm/1in lengths
   (about 1/2 cup)

225g/8oz/31/4 cups chestnut
   mushrooms, sliced

1 piece drained canned bamboo shoot,
   about 50g/2oz, shredded

5ml/1 tsp dried chilli flakes,
   to garnish (optional)

1 Cut up the guinea fowl, remove and discard the skin, then take all the meat off the bones. Chop the meat into bitesize pieces and set aside.

2 Heat the oil in a wok or frying pan and add the curry paste. Stir-fry over a medium heat for 30 seconds, until the paste gives off its aroma.

3 Add the fish sauce and the guinea fowl meat and stir-fry until the meat is browned all over. Add the galangal, peppercorns, lime leaves and whisky, then pour in the stock.

4 Bring to the boil. Add the vegetables, return to a simmer and cook gently for 2–3 minutes, until they are just cooked. Spoon into a dish, sprinkle with chilli flakes, if you like, and serve.

Nutritional information per portion: Energy 368Kcal/1540kJ; Protein 56.8g; Carbohydrate 1.4g, of which sugars 0.9g; Fat 14g, of which saturates 3.2g; Cholesterol 45mg; Calcium 82mg; Fibre 1.1g; Sodium 454mg.

Mussaman curry

This dish is traditionally based on beef, but chicken, lamb or tofu can be used instead. It has a rich, sweet and spicy flavour and is best served with boiled rice.

SERVES 4–6

600ml/1 pint/2¹/₂ cups coconut milk

675g/1¹/₂lb stewing steak, fat removed
    and cut into 2.5cm/1in chunks

250ml/8fl oz/1 cup coconut cream

45ml/3 tbsp Mussaman curry paste

30ml/2 tbsp Thai fish sauce

15ml/1 tbsp palm sugar (jaggery) or light
    muscovado (brown) sugar

60ml/4 tbsp tamarind juice (tamarind
    paste mixed with warm water)

6 green cardamom pods

1 cinnamon stick

1 large potato, about 225g/8oz,
    cut into even chunks

1 onion, cut into wedges

50g/2oz/¹/₂ cup roasted peanuts

1 Pour the coconut milk into a large, heavy pan and bring to the boil over a medium heat. Add the chunks of beef, reduce the heat to low, partially cover the pan and simmer gently for about 40 minutes, or until tender.

2 In a separate pan, heat the coconut cream and cook over a medium heat, stirring constantly, for about 5 minutes, or until it separates. Stir in the Mussaman curry paste and cook rapidly, stirring for 2–3 minutes.

3 Add the coconut cream and curry paste mixture to the pan with the beef and stir until thoroughly blended. Simmer for a further 4–5 minutes, stirring occasionally. Stir the rest of the ingredients, except the peanuts, into the curry. Simmer for 15–20 minutes, or until the potato is tender.

4 Add the roasted peanuts to the pan and mix well to combine. Cook for 5 minutes more, then transfer to warmed bowls and serve.

Nutritional information per portion: Energy 500Kcal/2095kJ; Protein 44.3g; Carbohydrate 24.4g, of which sugars 14.7g; Fat 25.7g, of which saturates 15g; Cholesterol 113mg; Calcium 75mg; Fibre 1.7g; Sodium 749mg.

Thick beef curry in sweet peanut sauce

This curry is deliciously rich and thicker than most other Thai curries, and is perfect served with boiled jasmine rice. Use salted duck's eggs for the garnish, if you can find them.

SERVES 4–6

600ml/1 pint/2¹/₂ cups coconut milk
45ml/3 tbsp Thai red curry paste
45ml/3 tbsp Thai fish sauce
30ml/2 tbsp palm sugar (jaggery) or
   light muscovado (brown) sugar
2 lemon grass stalks, bruised
450g/1lb rump (round) steak, cut into
   thin strips
75g/3oz/³/₄ cup roasted
   peanuts, ground
2 fresh red chillies, sliced
5 kaffir lime leaves, torn
salt and ground black pepper
2 salted eggs, cut in wedges, and 10–15
   Thai basil leaves, to garnish

1 Pour half the coconut milk into a large, heavy pan. Place over a medium heat and bring to the boil, stirring constantly until the milk separates.

2 Stir in the red curry paste and cook for 2–3 minutes until the mixture is fragrant and thoroughly blended. Add the fish sauce, sugar and bruised lemon grass stalks. Mix well.

3 Continue to cook until the colour deepens. Gradually add the remaining coconut milk, stirring constantly. Bring back to the boil.

4 Add the beef and peanuts. Cook, stirring constantly, for 8–10 minutes, or until most of the liquid has evaporated. Add the chillies and lime leaves. Season to taste and serve, garnished with wedges of salted eggs and Thai basil leaves.

Nutritional information per portion: Energy 310Kcal/1296kJ; Protein 29.1g; Carbohydrate 9.7g, of which sugars 8.5g; Fat 17.4g, of which saturates 5.3g; Cholesterol 69mg; Calcium 59mg; Fibre 1.2g; Sodium 215mg.

Green beef curry with Thai aubergines

The cooking time for this curry is very quick so be sure to use good quality meat. Sirloin is recommended, but tender rump (round) steak could be used instead.

SERVES 4–6

450g/1lb beef sirloin, excess fat removed
15ml/1 tbsp vegetable oil
45ml/3 tbsp Thai green curry paste
600ml/1 pint/2½ cups coconut milk
4 kaffir lime leaves, torn
15–30ml/1–2 tbsp Thai fish sauce
5ml/1 tsp palm sugar (jaggery) or
    light muscovado (brown) sugar
150g/5oz small Thai aubergines
    (eggplants), halved
small handful of fresh Thai basil
2 fresh green chillies, to garnish

1 Using a sharp knife, cut the beef into long, thin strips. Set aside.

2 Heat the oil in a large, heavy pan or wok. Add the curry paste and cook for 1–2 minutes, until fragrant.

3 Stir in half the coconut milk, a little at a time. Cook, stirring, for about 5–6 minutes, until an oily sheen appears on the surface.

4 Add the beef to the pan with the kaffir lime leaves, Thai fish sauce, sugar and aubergine halves. Cook for 2–3 minutes, then stir in the remaining coconut milk.

5 Bring back to a simmer and cook until the meat and aubergines are tender. Stir in the Thai basil just before serving. Finely shred the chillies and use to garnish the curry.

Nutritional information per portion: Energy 226Kcal/949kJ; Protein 24.7g; Carbohydrate 9.4g, of which sugars 9.3g; Fat 10.2g, of which saturates 3.8g; Cholesterol 69mg; Calcium 53mg; Fibre 0.8g; Sodium 393mg.

Stir-fried beef in oyster sauce

In Thailand this is often made with just straw mushrooms, which are readily available fresh, but oyster mushrooms make a good substitute and using a mixture makes the dish extra interesting.

SERVES 4–6

450g/1lb rump (round) steak
30ml/2 tbsp soy sauce
15ml/1 tbsp cornflour (cornstarch)
45ml/3 tbsp vegetable oil
15ml/1 tbsp chopped garlic
15ml/1 tbsp chopped fresh
   root ginger
225g/8oz/3¼ cups mixed mushrooms
   such as shiitake, oyster and straw
30ml/2 tbsp oyster sauce
5ml/1 tsp granulated (white) sugar
4 spring onions (scallions),
   cut into short lengths
ground black pepper
2 fresh red chillies, seeded and cut into
   strips, to garnish

1 Place the steak in the freezer for 30–40 minutes, then slice it on the diagonal into long thin strips.

2 Mix together the soy sauce and cornflour in a large bowl. Add the steak, turning to coat well, cover with clear film (plastic wrap) and leave to marinate for 1–2 hours.

3 Heat half the oil in a wok or frying pan. Add the garlic and ginger and cook for 1–2 minutes. Drain the steak, add to the wok and cook, stirring frequently, for a further 1–2 minutes.

4 When the steak is browned all over and tender, remove it from the wok and set aside.

5 Heat the remaining oil in the wok. Add the mushrooms. Stir-fry over a medium heat until golden brown. Return the beef to the wok and mix.

6 Spoon in the oyster sauce and sugar, mix well, add pepper to taste and toss until thoroughly combined. Stir in the spring onions. Transfer to a serving platter, garnish with the strips of red chilli and serve.

Nutritional information per portion: Energy 282Kcal/1177kJ; Protein 25.4g; Carbohydrate 10.7g, of which sugars 3.4g; Fat 15.5g, of which saturates 4.2g; Cholesterol 69mg; Calcium 16mg; Fibre 0.8g; Sodium 697mg.

Lemon grass pork

Chillies and lemon grass flavour this simple stir-fry, while crunchy peanuts add an interesting contrast in texture. Look out for jars of chopped lemon grass, which are handy to have in reserve when the fresh vegetable is not readily available.

SERVES 4

675g/1½lb boneless pork loin
2 lemon grass stalks, finely chopped
4 spring onions (scallions), thinly sliced
5ml/1 tsp salt
12 black peppercorns, coarsely crushed
30ml/2 tbsp groundnut (peanut) oil
2 garlic cloves, chopped
2 fresh red chillies, seeded and chopped

5ml/1 tsp soft light brown sugar
30ml/2 tbsp Thai fish sauce
25g/1oz/¼ cup roasted unsalted
   peanuts, chopped
ground black pepper
coarsely torn coriander (cilantro) leaves,
   to garnish
cooked rice noodles, to serve

1 Trim any excess fat from the pork. Cut the meat across into 5mm/¼in thick slices, then cut each slice into 5mm/¼in strips. Put the pork into a bowl with the lemon grass, spring onions, salt and crushed peppercorns and mix well. Cover with clear film (plastic wrap) and leave to marinate in a cool place for 30 minutes.

2 Preheat a wok, add the oil and swirl it around. Add the pork mixture and stir-fry over a medium heat for about 3 minutes, until browned all over.

3 Add the garlic and red chillies and stir-fry for a further 5–8 minutes over a medium heat, until the pork is cooked through and tender.

4 Add the sugar, Thai fish sauce and chopped peanuts and toss to mix, then season to taste with freshly ground black pepper. Serve immediately on a bed of rice noodles, garnished with the coarsely torn coriander leaves.

Nutritional information per portion: Energy 205Kcal/856kJ; Protein 27.9g; Carbohydrate 4.8g, of which sugars 1.6g; Fat 9.5g, of which saturates 2.4g; Cholesterol 78mg; Calcium 1.8mg; Fibre 0.4g; Sodium 88mg.

Pork and pineapple coconut curry

The heat of this curry balances out its sweetness to make a smooth and fragrant dish. It takes very little time to cook, so is ideal for a quick supper or for a mid-week family meal.

SERVES 4

400ml/14fl oz/1²/₃ coconut milk

10ml/2 tsp Thai red curry paste

400g/14oz pork loin steaks, trimmed and thinly sliced

15ml/1 tbsp Thai fish sauce

5ml/1 tsp palm sugar (jaggery) or light muscovado (brown) sugar

15ml/1 tbsp tamarind juice, made by mixing tamarind paste with warm water

2 kaffir lime leaves, torn

¹/₂ medium pineapple, peeled and chopped

1 fresh red chilli, seeded and finely chopped, to garnish

1 Pour the coconut milk into a bowl and let it settle, so that the cream rises to the surface. Scoop the cream into a measuring jug (cup). You should have about 250ml/8fl oz/1 cup. If necessary, add a little of the coconut milk.

2 Pour the coconut cream into a large pan and bring it to the boil. Cook for about 10 minutes, stirring frequently to prevent it from sticking, until the cream separates. Add the red curry paste and stir until well mixed. Cook, stirring occasionally, for about 4 minutes, until the paste is fragrant.

3 Add the sliced pork and stir in the fish sauce, sugar and tamarind juice. Cook for 1–2 minutes, until the sugar has dissolved and the pork is no longer pink.

4 Add the remaining coconut milk and the lime leaves. Bring to the boil, then stir in the pineapple. Reduce the heat and simmer gently for 3 minutes, or until the pork is fully cooked. Sprinkle over the chilli and serve.

Nutritional information per portion: Energy 191Kcal/807kJ; Protein 22.2g; Carbohydrate 16.4g, of which sugars 16.3g; Fat 4.5g, of which saturates 1.6g; Cholesterol 63mg; Calcium 55mg; Fibre 1.2g; Sodium 449mg.

Pork belly with five spices

The Chinese influence on Thai cuisine stems from the early years of its history, when colonists from southern China settled in the country, bringing with them dishes like this.

SERVES 4

large bunch fresh coriander (cilantro)
   with roots
30ml/2 tbsp vegetable oil
1 garlic clove, crushed
30ml/2 tbsp five-spice powder
500g/1¼lb pork belly, cut into
   2.5cm/1in pieces
400g/14oz can chopped tomatoes
150ml/¼ pint/⅔ cup hot water
30ml/2 tbsp dark soy sauce
45ml/3 tbsp Thai fish sauce
30ml/2 tbsp granulated (white) sugar
juice of 1 lime

1 Cut off the coriander roots. Chop five of them finely and freeze the remainder for another occasion. Chop the coriander stalks and leaves and set them aside. Keep the roots separate.

2 Heat the oil in a large pan and cook the garlic until golden brown. Stirring constantly, add the chopped coriander roots and then the five-spice powder.

3 Add the pork and stir-fry until the meat is thoroughly coated in spices and has browned. Stir in the tomatoes and hot water. Bring to the boil, then stir in the soy sauce, fish sauce and sugar.

4 Reduce the heat, cover the pan and simmer for 30 minutes. Stir in the chopped coriander stalks and leaves, sprinkle over the lime juice and serve.

Nutritional information per portion: Energy 426Kcal/1774kJ; Protein 26.1g; Carbohydrate 11g, of which sugars 10.6g; Fat 31.2g, of which saturates 9.8g; Cholesterol 89mg; Calcium 82mg; Fibre 2.2g; Sodium 936mg.

Curried pork with pickled garlic

This very rich curry is best accompanied by lots of plain rice and perhaps a light vegetable dish. It could serve four if served with a vegetable curry.

SERVES 2

130g/4¹/₂oz lean pork steaks
30ml/2 tbsp vegetable oil
1 garlic clove, crushed
15ml/1 tbsp Thai red curry paste
130ml/4¹/₂fl oz/generous ¹/₂ cup
    coconut cream
2.5cm/1in piece fresh root ginger,
    finely chopped
30ml/2 tbsp vegetable or
    chicken stock
30ml/2 tbsp Thai fish sauce
5ml/1 tsp granulated (white) sugar
2.5ml/¹/₂ tsp ground turmeric
10ml/2 tsp lemon juice
4 pickled garlic cloves,
    finely chopped
strips of lemon and lime rind,
    to garnish

1 Place the pork steaks in the freezer for 30–40 minutes, until firm, then, using a sharp knife, cut the meat into fine slivers, trimming off any excess fat.

2 Heat the oil in a wok or large, heavy frying pan and cook the garlic over a low to medium heat until golden brown. Do not let it burn. Add the curry paste and stir in well.

3 Add the coconut cream and stir until the liquid begins to reduce and thicken. Stir in the pork. Cook for 2 minutes more, until the pork is cooked through.

4 Add the ginger, stock, fish sauce, sugar and turmeric, stirring constantly, then add the lemon juice and pickled garlic. Spoon into bowls, garnish with strips of rind, and serve.

Nutritional information per portion: Energy 214Kcal/891kJ; Protein 14.6g; Carbohydrate 8g, of which sugars 7.9g; Fat 13.9g, of which saturates 2.4g; Cholesterol 41mg; Calcium 37mg; Fibre 0g; Sodium 1046mg.

Sweet and sour pork, Thai-style

It was the Chinese who originally created sweet and sour cooking, but the Thais also do it very well. This version has a fresher and cleaner flavour than the original.

SERVES 4

350g/12oz lean pork
30ml/2 tbsp vegetable oil
4 garlic cloves, thinly sliced
1 small red onion, sliced
30ml/2 tbsp Thai fish sauce
15ml/1 tbsp granulated (white) sugar
1 red (bell) pepper, seeded and diced
½ cucumber, seeded and sliced
2 plum tomatoes, cut into wedges
115g/4oz piece of pineapple, chopped
2 spring onions (scallions), chopped
ground black pepper

TO GARNISH
coriander (cilantro) leaves
spring onions (scallions), shredded

1 Place the pork in the freezer for 30–40 minutes, until firm. Using a sharp knife, cut it into thin strips.

2 Heat the oil in a wok or large frying pan. Add the garlic. Cook over a medium heat until golden, then add the pork and stir-fry for 4–5 minutes. Add the onion slices and toss to mix.

3 Add the fish sauce, sugar and pepper to taste. Toss the mixture over the heat for 3–4 minutes more.

4 Stir in the red pepper, cucumber, tomatoes, pineapple and spring onions. Stir-fry for 3–4 minutes more, then spoon into a bowl. Garnish with the coriander and spring onions and serve.

Nutritional information per portion: Energy 214Kcal/894kJ; Protein 20.3g; Carbohydrate 12.5g, of which sugars 11.9g; Fat 9.5g, of which saturates 2g; Cholesterol 55mg; Calcium 34mg; Fibre 2g; Sodium 337mg.

Vegetable dishes

Many of the vegetable dishes in this chapter feature a large number of ingredients, and they are often served as main courses, but can also be adapted for use as side dishes. Delicious curries, unusual stir-fries, stuffed vegetables and a tasty tempura are included. The Thai preference for cooking fresh ingredients quickly, preserving plenty of flavour, is much in evidence here.

Tofu and green bean red curry

This is one of those versatile recipes that should be in every cook's repertoire. This version uses green beans, but other types of vegetable work equally well. The tofu takes on the flavour of the spice paste and also boosts the nutritional value.

SERVES 4–6

600ml/1 pint/2¹/₂ cups canned
coconut milk
15ml/1 tbsp Thai red curry paste
45ml/3 tbsp Thai fish sauce
10ml/2 tsp palm sugar (jaggery) or light
muscovado (brown) sugar
225g/8oz/3¹/₄ cups button
(white) mushrooms
115g/4oz/scant 1 cup green
beans, trimmed
175g/6oz firm tofu, rinsed, drained and
cut in 2cm/³/₄in cubes
4 kaffir lime leaves, torn
2 fresh red chillies, seeded and sliced
fresh coriander (cilantro) leaves, to garnish

1 Pour about one-third of the coconut milk into a wok or pan. Cook the coconut milk until it starts to separate and an oily sheen appears on the surface.

2 Add the red curry paste, fish sauce and sugar to the coconut milk. Mix well, then add the mushrooms. Stir and cook for 1 minute.

3 Stir in the remaining coconut milk. Bring back to the boil, then add the green beans and tofu cubes. Simmer gently for 4–5 minutes more.

4 Stir in the kaffir lime leaves and sliced red chillies. Spoon the curry into a serving dish, garnish with the fresh coriander leaves and serve immediately.

Nutritional information per portion: Energy 110Kcal/460kJ; Protein 5.7g; Carbohydrate 10.2g, of which sugars 9.6g; Fat 5.5g, of which saturates 0.9g; Cholesterol 0mg; Calcium 282mg; Fibre 1.3g; Sodium 437mg.

Vegetable forest curry

This is a thin, soupy curry with lots of fresh green vegetables and robust flavours. In the forested regions of Thailand, where it originated, it would be made using edible wild leaves and roots. Serve it with rice or noodles for a simple lunch or supper.

SERVES 2

600ml/1 pint/2¹/₂ cups water
5ml/1 tsp Thai red curry paste
5cm/2in piece fresh galangal
  or fresh root ginger
90g/3¹/₂oz/scant 1 cup green beans
2 kaffir lime leaves, torn
8 baby corn cobs, halved widthways
2 heads Chinese broccoli, chopped
90g/3¹/₂oz/generous 3 cups beansprouts
15ml/1 tbsp drained bottled green
  peppercorns, crushed
10ml/2 tsp granulated (white) sugar
5ml/1 tsp salt

1 Heat the water in a large pan. Add the red curry paste and stir until it is well blended in. Bring to the boil.

2 Meanwhile, using a sharp knife, peel and finely chop the fresh galangal or root ginger.

3 Add the galangal or ginger, green beans, lime leaves, baby corn cobs, broccoli and beansprouts to the pan.

4 Stir in the crushed peppercorns, sugar and salt. Bring to the boil, then reduce the heat to low and simmer for 2 minutes. Serve immediately.

Nutritional information per portion: Energy 107Kcal/448kJ; Protein 11g; Carbohydrate 11.3g, of which sugars 9.4g; Fat 2.2g, of which saturates 0.5g; Cholesterol 0mg; Calcium 129mg; Fibre 6.8g; Sodium 1427mg.

Corn and cashew nut curry

A substantial curry, this combines all the essential flavours of southern Thailand. It is deliciously aromatic, but the flavour is fairly mild.

SERVES 4

30ml/2 tbsp vegetable oil

4 shallots, chopped

90g/3¹/₂oz/scant 1 cup cashew nuts

5ml/1 tsp Thai red curry paste

400g/14oz potatoes, peeled and cut into chunks

1 lemon grass stalk, finely chopped

200g/7oz can chopped tomatoes

600ml/1 pint/2¹/₂ cups boiling water

200g/7oz/generous 1 cup drained canned whole kernel corn

4 celery sticks, sliced

2 kaffir lime leaves, thinly sliced

15ml/1 tbsp tomato ketchup

15ml/1 tbsp light soy sauce

5ml/1 tsp palm sugar (jaggery) or light muscovado (brown) sugar

5ml/1 tsp Thai fish sauce

4 spring onions (scallions), thinly sliced, and a small bunch fresh basil, chopped, to garnish

1 Heat the oil in a large, heavy frying pan or wok. Add the shallots and stir-fry them over a medium heat for 2–3 minutes, until they are softened. Add the cashew nuts and stir-fry for a few minutes until they are golden.

2 Stir in the red curry paste. Stir-fry for 1 minute, then add the potatoes, lemon grass, tomatoes and boiling water to the frying pan or wok.

3 Bring back to the boil, then reduce the heat to low, cover and simmer gently for 15–20 minutes, or until the potatoes are tender.

4 Stir in the corn, celery, lime leaves, tomato ketchup, soy sauce, sugar and fish sauce. Simmer for a further 5 minutes, until heated through, then spoon into warmed serving bowls. Sprinkle with the sliced spring onions and basil and serve.

Nutritional information per portion: Energy 342Kcal/1431kJ; Protein 8.7g; Carbohydrate 38.4g, of which sugars 12g; Fat 18.1g, of which saturates 3.2g; Cholesterol 0mg; Calcium 37mg; Fibre 3.5g; Sodium 564mg.

Sweet pumpkin and peanut curry

Hearty and soothing, this curry is perfect for cold autumn or winter evenings. Its cheerful colour alone will brighten you up – and it tastes terrific.

SERVES 4

30ml/2 tbsp vegetable oil

4 garlic cloves, crushed

4 shallots, finely chopped

30ml/2 tbsp yellow curry paste

600ml/1 pint/2½ cups vegetable stock

2 kaffir lime leaves, torn

15ml/1 tbsp chopped fresh galangal

450g/1lb pumpkin, peeled,
    seeded and diced

225g/8oz sweet potatoes, diced

90g/3½oz/scant 1 cup peanuts,
    roasted and chopped

300ml/½ pint/1¼ cups coconut milk

90g/3½oz/1½ cups chestnut
    mushrooms, sliced

15ml/1 tbsp soy sauce

30ml/2 tbsp Thai fish sauce

50g/2oz/⅓ cup pumpkin
    seeds, toasted, and fresh green chilli
    flowers (see page 213), to garnish

1 Heat the oil in a large pan. Add the garlic and shallots and cook over a medium heat, stirring occasionally, for 10 minutes, until softened and golden. Do not let them burn.

2 Add the yellow curry paste and stir-fry over a medium heat for 30 seconds, until fragrant, then add the stock, lime leaves, galangal, pumpkin and sweet potatoes.

3 Bring to the boil, stirring frequently, then reduce the heat to low and simmer gently for 15 minutes.

4 Add the peanuts, coconut milk and mushrooms. Stir in the soy sauce and fish sauce and simmer for 5 minutes more. Spoon into warmed individual serving bowls, garnish with the pumpkin seeds and chilli flowers and serve.

Nutritional information per portion: Energy 292Kcal/1218kJ; Protein 8.4g; Carbohydrate 22.2g, of which sugars 11.2g; Fat 19.5g, of which saturates 3.3g; Cholesterol 0mg; Calcium 87mg; Fibre 4.3g; Sodium 768mg.

Thai vegetable curry
with **lemon grass rice**

Fragrant jasmine rice, subtly flavoured with lemon grass and cardamom, is the perfect accompaniment for this richly spiced vegetable curry.

SERVES 4

10ml/2 tsp vegetable oil
400ml/14fl oz/1²/₃ cups coconut milk
300ml/¹/₂ pint/1¹/₄ cups
   vegetable stock
225g/8oz new potatoes, halved or
   quartered, if large
8 baby corn cobs
5ml/1 tsp golden caster (superfine) sugar
185g/6¹/₂oz/1¹/₄ cups broccoli florets
1 red (bell) pepper, seeded and
   sliced lengthways
115g/4oz spinach, tough stalks removed,
   leaves shredded
30ml/2 tbsp chopped fresh
   coriander (cilantro)
salt and ground black pepper

FOR THE SPICE PASTE
1 fresh red chilli, seeded
   and chopped
3 fresh green chillies, seeded
   and chopped

1 lemon grass stalk, outer leaves
   removed and lower 5cm/2in finely
   chopped
2 shallots, chopped
finely grated rind of 1 lime
2 garlic cloves, chopped
5ml/1 tsp ground coriander
2.5ml/¹/₂ tsp ground cumin
1cm/¹/₂in piece fresh galangal, peeled
   and finely chopped, or 2.5ml/¹/₂ tsp
   dried galangal (optional)
30ml/2 tbsp chopped fresh
   coriander (cilantro)
15ml/1 tbsp chopped fresh coriander
   (cilantro) roots and stems (optional)

FOR THE RICE
225g/8oz/1¹/₄ cups jasmine
   rice, rinsed
6 cardamom pods, bruised
1 lemon grass stalk, outer leaves
   removed, cut into 3 pieces
475ml/16fl oz/2 cups water

1 Make the spice paste. Place all the ingredients in a food processor and process to a coarse paste. Heat the oil in a large, heavy pan. Add the paste and stir-fry over a medium heat for 1–2 minutes.

2 Pour in the coconut milk and stock and bring to the boil. Reduce the heat, add the potatoes and simmer gently for about 15 minutes, until almost tender.

3 Meanwhile, put the rice into a large pan with the cardamoms and lemon grass. Pour in the water. Bring to the boil, reduce the heat, cover and cook for 10–15 minutes, until the water has been absorbed and the rice is tender and slightly sticky.

4 When the rice is cooked and slightly sticky, season to taste with salt, then replace the lid and leave to stand for about 10 minutes.

5 Add the baby corn to the potatoes, season with salt and pepper to taste, then cook for 2 minutes. Stir in the sugar, broccoli and red pepper and cook for 2 minutes, or until the vegetables are tender.

6 Stir the shredded spinach and half the fresh coriander into the vegetable mixture. Cook for 2 minutes, then spoon the curry into a warmed serving dish.

7 Remove and discard the cardamom pods and lemon grass from the rice and fluff up the grains with a fork. Garnish the curry with the remaining fresh coriander and serve with the rice.

Nutritional information per portion: Energy 441Kcal/1867kJ; Protein 11.2g; Carbohydrate 91g, of which sugars 33g; Fat 6.1g, of which saturates 1.4g; Cholesterol 58mg; Calcium 212mg; Fibre 0.3g; Sodium 594mg.

Mushrooms with garlic and chilli sauce

When you are planning a barbecue, it can be tricky finding something really special for vegetarians. These tasty kebabs are ideal because they look, smell and taste wonderful.

SERVES 4

12 large field (portobello), chestnut
   or oyster mushrooms or a mixture,
   cut in half
4 garlic cloves, coarsely chopped
6 coriander (cilantro) roots,
   coarsely chopped
15ml/1 tbsp granulated (white) sugar
30ml/2 tbsp light soy sauce
ground black pepper

FOR THE DIPPING SAUCE

15ml/1 tbsp granulated (white) sugar
90ml/6 tbsp rice vinegar
5ml/1 tsp salt
1 garlic clove, crushed
1 small fresh red chilli, seeded
   and finely chopped

1 Soak eight wooden skewers in water for 30 minutes, to prevent burning. Make the dipping sauce by heating the sugar, rice vinegar and salt in a small pan, stirring occasionally until the sugar and salt have dissolved. Add the garlic and chilli, pour into a serving dish and keep warm.

2 Thread the mushroom halves on to the skewers, putting three halves on each skewer. Lay the filled skewers side by side in a shallow dish.

3 In a mortar or spice grinder pound or blend the garlic and coriander roots. Scrape into a bowl and mix with the sugar, soy sauce and a little pepper.

4 Brush the soy sauce mixture over the mushrooms and leave to marinate for 15 minutes. Prepare the barbecue or preheat the grill (broiler) and cook the mushrooms for 2–3 minutes on each side. Serve with the dipping sauce.

Nutritional information per portion: Energy 40Kcal/167kJ; Protein 3.6g; Carbohydrate 4.5g, of which sugars 4.1g; Fat 1g, of which saturates 0.2g; Cholesterol 0mg; Calcium 14mg; Fibre 2.1g; Sodium 1035mg.

Stir-fried crispy tofu

The asparagus grown in Asia tends to have slender stalks. Look for it in Thai markets or substitute the thin asparagus popularly known as sprue.

SERVES 2

250g/9oz fried tofu cubes
30ml/2 tbsp groundnut (peanut) oil
15ml/1 tbsp Thai green curry paste
30ml/2 tbsp light soy sauce
2 kaffir lime leaves, rolled into cylinders
    and thinly sliced
30ml/2 tbsp granulated (white) sugar
150ml/¼ pint/⅔ cup vegetable stock
250g/9oz asparagus, trimmed and sliced
    into 5cm/2in lengths
30ml/2 tbsp roasted peanuts,
    finely chopped

1 Preheat the grill (broiler) to medium. Place the tofu cubes in a grill pan and grill (broil) for 2–3 minutes, then turn them over and continue to cook until they are crisp and golden brown all over.

2 Heat the oil in a wok or heavy frying pan. Add the green curry paste and cook over a medium heat, stirring, for 1–2 minutes, until it gives off its aroma.

3 Stir the soy sauce, lime leaves, sugar and vegetable stock into the wok or pan and mix well. Bring to the boil, then reduce the heat to low so that the mixture is just simmering.

4 Add the asparagus and simmer gently for 5 minutes. Meanwhile, chop each piece of tofu into four, then add to the pan with the peanuts.

5 Toss to coat all the ingredients in the sauce, and serve immediately.

Nutritional information per portion: Energy 510Kcal/2122kJ; Protein 33.5g; Carbohydrate 18.8g, of which sugars 17.2g; Fat 33.9g, of which saturates 2.2g; Cholesterol 0mg; Calcium 1893mg; Fibre 2.2g; Sodium 1085mg.

Aubergine and sweet potato stew with coconut milk

Scented with fragrant lemon grass, ginger and lots of garlic, this hearty stew contains a particularly good combination of flavours. Aubergines and sweet potatoes go perfectly together while the creamy coconut milk adds a mellow note.

SERVES 6

400g/14oz baby aubergines (eggplants) or 2 standard aubergines

60ml/4 tbsp groundnut (peanut) oil

225g/8oz Thai red shallots or other small shallots or pickling onions

5ml/1 tsp fennel seeds, lightly crushed

4–5 garlic cloves, thinly sliced

25ml/1½ tbsp finely chopped fresh root ginger

475ml/16fl oz/2 cups vegetable stock

2 lemon grass stalks, outer layers discarded, finely chopped

15g/½oz/⅔ cup fresh coriander (cilantro), stalks and leaves chopped separately

3 kaffir lime leaves, lightly bruised

2–3 small fresh red chillies

45–60ml/3–4 tbsp Thai green curry paste

675g/1½lb sweet potatoes, peeled and cut into thick chunks

400ml/14fl oz/1⅔ cups coconut milk

2.5–5ml/½–1 tsp palm sugar (jaggery) or light muscovado (brown) sugar

250g/9oz/3½ cups mushrooms, thickly sliced

juice of 1 lime, to taste

salt and ground black pepper

fresh Thai basil leaves, to garnish

boiled rice, to serve

1 Trim the aubergines. If using baby aubergines, slice in half lengthways. Cut standard-sized aubergines into chunks.

2 Heat half the oil in a wide pan or deep, lidded frying pan. Add the aubergines and cook (uncovered) over a medium heat, stirring occasionally, until lightly browned on all sides. Remove from the pan and set aside.

3 Slice 4–5 of the shallots. Cook the whole shallots in the oil remaining in the pan, adding a little more oil if necessary, until lightly browned. Set aside with the aubergines. Add the remaining oil to the pan and cook the sliced shallots, fennel seeds, garlic and ginger over a low heat for 5 minutes.

4 Add the stock, lemon grass, chopped coriander stalks and any roots, lime leaves and whole chillies. Bring to the boil, cover and simmer over a low heat for 5 minutes.

5 Stir in 30ml/2 tbsp of the curry paste and the sweet potatoes. Simmer gently for 10 minutes, then return the aubergines and browned shallots to the pan and cook for a further 5 minutes.

6 Stir in the coconut milk and the sugar. Season to taste with salt and pepper, then stir in the mushrooms and simmer gently for 5 minutes, or until all the vegetables are cooked and tender.

7 Stir in more curry paste and lime juice to taste, followed by the chopped coriander leaves. Adjust the seasoning, if necessary, and ladle the vegetables into warmed bowls. Sprinkle basil leaves over the stew and serve with rice.

Nutritional information per portion: Energy 236Kcal/992kJ; Protein 3.5g; Carbohydrate 30.2g, of which sugars 12.4g; Fat 12.2g, of which saturates 2.2g; Cholesterol 0mg; Calcium 65mg; Fibre 5g; Sodium 210mg.

Sweet and sour vegetables with tofu

Big, bold and colourful, this is a nutritious stir-fry with plenty of flavour. Stir-fries are always a good choice when entertaining as you can prepare the ingredients ahead of time.

SERVES 4

4 shallots
3 garlic cloves
30ml/2 tbsp groundnut (peanut) oil
250g/9oz Chinese leaves (Chinese cabbage), shredded
8 baby corn cobs, sliced on the diagonal
2 red (bell) peppers, thinly sliced
200g/7oz/1¾ cups mangetouts (snow peas), trimmed and sliced
250g/9oz tofu, rinsed, drained and cut in 1cm/½in cubes
60ml/4 tbsp vegetable stock
30ml/2 tbsp light soy sauce
15ml/1 tbsp granulated (white) sugar
30ml/2 tbsp rice vinegar
2.5ml/½ tsp dried chilli flakes
small bunch coriander (cilantro), chopped

1 Slice the shallots thinly using a sharp knife. Finely chop the garlic.

2 Heat the oil in a wok or large frying pan and cook the shallots and garlic for 2–3 minutes over a medium heat, until golden. Do not let the garlic burn.

3 Add the shredded cabbage, toss over the heat for 30 seconds, then add the sliced corn cobs and repeat the process.

4 Add the red peppers, mangetouts and tofu in the same way, each time adding a single ingredient and tossing it over the heat for about 30 seconds before adding the next ingredient.

5 Pour in the stock and soy sauce. Mix together the sugar and vinegar in a small bowl, stirring until the sugar has dissolved, then add to the wok or pan. Sprinkle over the chilli flakes and coriander, toss to mix well and serve.

Nutritional information per portion: Energy 177Kcal/736kJ; Protein 10.5g; Carbohydrate 13.7g, of which sugars 12.5g; Fat 9.2g, of which saturates 1.5g; Cholesterol 0mg; Calcium 461mg; Fibre 4.3g; Sodium 844mg.

Snake beans with tofu

Another name for snake beans is yard-long beans. This is something of an exaggeration but they do grow to lengths of 35cm/14in and more. If you cannot find any, substitute other green beans.

SERVES 4

500g/1¼lb long beans, thinly sliced
200g/7oz silken tofu, cut into cubes
2 shallots, thinly sliced
200ml/7fl oz/scant 1 cup
    coconut milk
115g/4oz/1 cup roasted
    peanuts, chopped
juice of 1 lime
10ml/2 tsp palm sugar (jaggery) or
    light muscovado (brown) sugar
60ml/4 tbsp soy sauce
5ml/1 tsp dried chilli flakes

1 Bring a pan of lightly salted water to the boil. Add the beans and blanch them for 30 seconds.

2 Drain the beans immediately, then refresh under cold water and drain again, shaking well to remove as much water as possible. Place in a serving bowl and set aside.

3 Put the tofu and shallots in a pan with the coconut milk. Heat gently, stirring, until the tofu begins to crumble.

4 Add the peanuts, lime juice, sugar, soy sauce and chilli flakes. Heat, stirring, until the sugar has dissolved.

5 Pour the sauce over the beans, toss to combine and serve immediately.

Nutritional information per portion: Energy 263Kcal/1091kJ; Protein 14.5g; Carbohydrate 13.3g, of which sugars 10g; Fat 17.2g, of which saturates 3g; Cholesterol 0mg; Calcium 335mg; Fibre 4.7g; Sodium 1353mg.

Tofu and vegetable Thai curry

Traditional Thai ingredients – chillies, galangal, lemon grass and kaffir lime leaves – give this curry a wonderfully fragrant aroma. The tofu needs to marinate for at least 2 hours to soak up all the delicious flavours, so bear this in mind when timing your meal.

SERVES 4

175g/6oz firm tofu
45ml/3 tbsp dark soy sauce
15ml/1 tbsp sesame oil
5ml/1 tsp chilli sauce
2.5cm/1in piece fresh root ginger, peeled
    and finely grated
1 head broccoli, about 225g/8oz
1/2 head cauliflower, about 225g/8oz
30ml/2 tbsp vegetable oil
1 onion, sliced
400ml/14fl oz/1²/₃ cups coconut milk
150ml/1/4 pint/²/₃ cup water
1 red (bell) pepper, seeded
    and chopped
175g/6oz/generous 1 cup green
    beans, halved
115g/4oz/1¹/₂ cups shiitake or button
    (white) mushrooms, halved

shredded spring onions (scallions),
    to garnish
boiled jasmine rice or noodles,
    to serve

FOR THE CURRY PASTE
2 fresh red or green chillies, seeded
    and chopped
1 lemon grass stalk, chopped
2.5cm/1in piece fresh
    galangal, peeled and chopped
2 kaffir lime leaves
10ml/2 tsp ground coriander
a few fresh coriander (cilantro) sprigs,
    including the stalks
45ml/3 tbsp water

1 Rinse and drain the tofu. Using a sharp knife, cut it into 2.5cm/1in cubes. Place the cubes in an ovenproof dish that is large enough to hold them all in a single layer.

2 Mix together the soy sauce, sesame oil, chilli sauce and grated ginger in a jug (pitcher) and pour over the tofu. Toss gently to coat all the cubes evenly, cover with clear film (plastic wrap) and leave to marinate for at least 2 hours or overnight if possible, turning and basting the tofu occasionally.

3 To make the curry paste, place the chillies, lemon grass, galangal, lime leaves, ground coriander and fresh coriander in a food processor and process until blended. Add the water and process to a thick paste.

4 Preheat the oven to 190°C/375°F/Gas 5. Cut the broccoli and cauliflower into small florets. Cut any stalks into thin slices.

5 Heat the vegetable oil in a frying pan and add the sliced onion. Cook over a low heat for about 8 minutes, until soft and lightly browned. Stir in the curry paste and the coconut milk. Add the water and bring to the boil.

6 Stir in the red pepper, green beans, broccoli and cauliflower. Transfer to a casserole. Cover and place towards the bottom of the oven.

7 Stir the tofu and marinade, then place the dish on a shelf near the top of the oven. Cook for 30 minutes. Remove both the dish and the casserole from the oven. Add the tofu, with any remaining marinade, to the curry, with the mushrooms, and stir well.

8 Return the casserole to the oven, reduce the temperature to 180°C/350°F/Gas 4 and cook for about 15 minutes, or until the vegetables are tender. Garnish with the spring onions and serve with the rice or noodles.

Nutritional information per portion: Energy 210Kcal/873kJ; Protein 11g; Carbohydrate 15.1g, of which sugars 13.3g; Fat 12g, of which saturates 1.8g; Cholesterol 0mg; Calcium 328mg; Fibre 5g; Sodium 927mg.

Stir-fried seeds and vegetables

The contrast between the crunchy seeds and vegetables and the rich, savoury sauce is what makes this dish so delicious. Serve it solo, or with rice or noodles.

SERVES 4

30ml/2 tbsp vegetable oil

30ml/2 tbsp sesame seeds

30ml/2 tbsp sunflower seeds

30ml/2 tbsp pumpkin seeds

2 garlic cloves, finely chopped

2.5cm/1in piece fresh root ginger, peeled and finely chopped

2 large carrots, cut into batons

2 large courgettes (zucchini), cut into batons

90g/3½oz/1½ cups oyster mushrooms, torn in pieces

150g/5oz watercress or spinach leaves, coarsely chopped

small bunch fresh mint or coriander (cilantro), leaves and stems chopped

60ml/4 tbsp black bean sauce

30ml/2 tbsp light soy sauce

15ml/1 tbsp palm sugar (jaggery) or light muscovado (brown) sugar

30ml/2 tbsp rice vinegar

1 Heat the oil in a wok or large frying pan. Add the seeds. Toss over a medium heat for 1 minute, then add the garlic and ginger and continue to stir-fry until the ginger is aromatic and the garlic is golden. Do not let the garlic burn or it will taste bitter.

2 Add the carrot and courgette batons and the mushroom pieces to the wok or pan and stir-fry over a medium heat for a further 5 minutes.

3 When all the vegetables are crisp-tender and golden at the edges, add the watercress or spinach to the wok or pan with the mint or coriander.

4 Toss over the heat for 1 minute, then stir in the black bean sauce, soy sauce, sugar and vinegar.

5 Continue to stir-fry for 1–2 minutes, until combined and hot. Serve immediately.

Nutritional information per portion: Energy 248Kcal/1030kJ; Protein 7.6g; Carbohydrate 12g, of which sugars 9.2g; Fat 19.1g, of which saturates 2.5g; Cholesterol 0mg; Calcium 238mg; Fibre 3.2g; Sodium 743mg.

Stuffed sweet peppers

This is an unusual recipe in that the stuffed peppers are steamed rather than baked. The filling incorporates typical Thai ingredients such as red curry paste and fish sauce.

SERVES 4

3 garlic cloves, finely chopped

2 coriander (cilantro) roots, finely chopped

400g/14oz/3 cups mushrooms, quartered

5ml/1 tsp Thai red curry paste

1 egg, lightly beaten

15ml/1 tbsp Thai fish sauce

15ml/1 tbsp light soy sauce

2.5ml/¹/₂ tsp granulated (white) sugar

3 kaffir lime leaves, finely chopped

4 yellow (bell) peppers, halved lengthways and seeded

1 In a mortar or spice grinder pound or blend the garlic with the coriander roots. Scrape into a bowl.

2 Put the mushrooms in a food processor and pulse briefly until they are finely chopped. Add to the garlic mixture, then stir in the curry paste, egg, fish sauce, soy sauce, sugar and lime leaves.

3 Place the pepper halves in a single layer in a steamer basket. Spoon the mixture loosely into the pepper halves. Do not pack the mixture down tightly or the filling will dry out too much.

4 Bring the water in the steamer to the boil, then lower to a simmer. Steam the peppers for 15 minutes, or until the flesh is tender. Serve hot.

Nutritional information per portion: Energy 100Kcal/417kJ; Protein 5.5g; Carbohydrate 12g, of which sugars 11.3g; Fat 3.6g, of which saturates 0.8g; Cholesterol 55mg; Calcium 29mg; Fibre 3.9g; Sodium 388mg.

Aubergine and pepper tempura with sweet chilli dip

Although tempura is a signature dish of Japanese cuisine, it has now also become popular throughout Asia, with each country adding its own characteristic touch – which in the case of Thailand is this chilli-flavoured sauce.

SERVES 4

2 aubergines (eggplants)
2 red (bell) peppers, halved and seeded
vegetable oil, for deep-frying

FOR THE TEMPURA BATTER
250g/9oz/2¼ cups plain
    (all-purpose) flour
2 egg yolks
500ml/17fl oz/2¼ cups iced water
5ml/1 tsp salt

FOR THE DIP
150ml/¼ pint/⅔ cup water
10ml/2 tsp granulated (white) sugar
1 fresh red chilli, seeded and
    finely chopped
1 garlic clove, crushed
juice of ½ lime
5ml/1 tsp rice vinegar
35ml/2½ tbsp Thai fish sauce
½ small carrot, finely grated

1 Slice the aubergines into thin batons. Slice the red peppers thinly.

2 Make the dip. Mix together all the ingredients in a bowl and stir until the sugar has dissolved. Cover with clear film (plastic wrap) and set aside.

3 Pour the oil into a large pan, wok or deep-fryer and gently heat to 190°C/375°F or until a cube of bread, added to the oil, browns in about 30 seconds.

4 Meanwhile, make the tempura batter. Set aside 30ml/2 tbsp of the flour. Put the egg yolks in a large bowl and beat in the iced water. Add the remaining flour with the salt and stir briefly together – the mixture should resemble thick pancake batter but be lumpy and not properly mixed. If it is too thick, add a little more iced water. Do not leave the batter to stand; use it immediately.

5 Pick up a small handful of aubergine batons and pepper slices, dust with the reserved flour, then dip into the batter.

6 Drop into the hot oil, taking care as the oil will froth up furiously. Repeat to make two or three more fritters, but do not cook any more than this at one time, or the oil may overflow.

7 Cook the fritters for 3–4 minutes, until they are golden and crisp all over, then lift them out with a metal basket or slotted spoon. Drain thoroughly on kitchen paper and keep hot.

8 Repeat until all the vegetables have been coated in batter and cooked. Serve immediately, with the dip.

Nutritional information per portion: Energy 442Kcal/1856kJ; Protein 9.5g; Carbohydrate 57.7g, of which sugars 9.6g; Fat 20.9g, of which saturates 3.1g; Cholesterol 101mg; Calcium 122mg; Fibre 6.2g; Sodium 859mg.

Thai asparagus

This is an excitingly different way of cooking asparagus. The crunchy texture is retained and the flavour is complemented by the addition of galangal and chilli.

SERVES 4

350g/12oz asparagus stalks

30ml/2 tbsp vegetable oil

1 garlic clove, crushed

15ml/1 tbsp sesame seeds, toasted

2.5cm/1in piece fresh galangal, finely shredded

1 fresh red chilli, seeded and peeled and finely chopped

15ml/1 tbsp Thai fish sauce

15ml/1 tbsp light soy sauce

45ml/3 tbsp water

5ml/1 tsp palm sugar (jaggery) or light muscovado (brown) sugar

1 Snap the asparagus stalks. They will break naturally at the junction between the woody base and the more tender portion of the stalk. Discard the woody parts of the stems.

2 Heat the oil in a wok and stir-fry the garlic, sesame seeds and galangal for 3–4 seconds, until the garlic is just beginning to turn golden.

3 Add the asparagus stalks and chilli, toss to mix, then add the fish sauce, soy sauce, water and sugar. Using two spoons, toss over the heat for a further 2 minutes, or until the asparagus just begins to soften and the liquid is reduced by half.

4 Carefully transfer to a warmed platter and serve immediately.

Nutritional information per portion: Energy 120Kcal/492kJ; Protein 4.1g; Carbohydrate 2.4g, of which sugars 2.3g; Fat 10.4g, of which saturates 1.4g; Cholesterol 0mg; Calcium 75mg; Fibre 2.1g; Sodium 537mg.

Fragrant mushrooms in lettuce leaves

This quick and easy vegetable dish is served on lettuce leaf "saucers" so can be eaten with the fingers – a great treat for children.

SERVES 2

30ml/2 tbsp vegetable oil

2 garlic cloves, finely chopped

2 baby cos or romaine lettuces,
   or 2 Little Gem (Bibb) lettuces

1 lemon grass stalk, finely chopped

2 kaffir lime leaves, rolled in cylinders
   and thinly sliced

200g/7oz/3 cups oyster or chestnut
   mushrooms, sliced

1 small fresh red chilli, seeded
   and finely chopped

juice of ½ lemon

30ml/2 tbsp light soy sauce

5ml/1 tsp palm sugar (jaggery) or light
   muscovado (brown) sugar

small bunch fresh mint, leaves removed
   from the stalks

1 Heat the oil in a wok or frying pan. Add the garlic and cook over a medium heat, stirring occasionally, until golden. Do not let the garlic burn or it will taste bitter.

2 Meanwhile, separate the individual lettuce leaves and set aside.

3 Increase the heat under the wok or pan and add the lemon grass, lime leaves and sliced mushrooms. Stir-fry for about 2 minutes.

4 Add the chilli, lemon juice, soy sauce and sugar to the wok or pan. Toss the mixture over the heat to combine the ingredients together, then stir-fry for a further 2 minutes.

5 Arrange the lettuce leaves on a large plate. Spoon a small amount of the mushroom mixture on to each leaf, top with a mint leaf and serve.

Nutritional information per portion: Energy 133Kcal/548kJ; Protein 3.1g; Carbohydrate 3.4g, of which sugars 3g; Fat 12g, of which saturates 1.5g; Cholesterol 0mg; Calcium 37mg; Fibre 2g; Sodium 1076mg.

Fried vegetables with nam prik

Nam prik is the universal Thai sauce. It can be served as a condiment, but it is more often used as a dip for fresh or cooked vegetables.

SERVES 4

3 large (US extra large) eggs

1 aubergine (eggplant), halved lengthways and cut into long, thin slices

$1/2$ small butternut squash, peeled, seeded and cut into long, thin slices

2 courgettes (zucchini), trimmed and cut into long, thin slices

105ml/7 tbsp vegetable or sunflower oil

salt and ground black pepper

nam prik or sweet chilli sauce, to serve

1 Beat the eggs in a large bowl. Add the aubergine, butternut squash and courgette slices. Toss until coated all over in egg, then season.

2 Heat the oil in a wok. When it is hot, add the vegetables, one strip at a time, making sure that each strip is coated in the egg. Do not cook more than eight strips at a time or the oil will cool down too much.

3 As each strip turns golden and is cooked, lift it out, using a wire basket or slotted spoon, and drain on kitchen paper. Keep hot while cooking the rest of the vegetables.

4 When all the vegetables are cooked, transfer them to a warmed dish and serve with the nam prik or sweet chilli sauce as a dip.

Nutritional information per portion: Energy 90Kcal/378kJ; Protein 10.1g; Carbohydrate 8.4g, of which sugars 7.1g; Fat 2g, of which saturates 0.4g; Cholesterol 95mg; Calcium 111mg; Fibre 6.3g; Sodium 1010mg.

Pak choi with lime dressing

The coconut dressing for this Thai speciality is traditionally made using fish sauce, but vegetarians could use mushroom sauce instead. Beware, this is a fiery dish!

SERVES 4

30ml/2 tbsp vegetable oil

3 fresh red chillies, cut into thin strips

4 garlic cloves, thinly sliced

6 spring onions (scallions), sliced diagonally

2 pak choi (bok choy), shredded

15ml/1 tbsp crushed peanuts

FOR THE DRESSING

30ml/2 tbsp fresh lime juice

15–30ml/1–2 tbsp Thai fish sauce

250ml/8fl oz/1 cup coconut milk

1 Make the dressing. Put the lime juice and fish sauce in a bowl and mix well together, then gradually whisk in the coconut milk.

2 Heat the oil in a wok and stir-fry the chillies for 2–3 minutes, until crisp. Transfer to a plate using a slotted spoon. Add the garlic to the wok and stir-fry for 30–60 seconds, until golden brown. Transfer to the plate.

3 Stir-fry the white parts of the spring onions for about 2–3 minutes, then add the green parts and stir-fry for 1 minute more. Transfer to the plate.

4 Bring a large pan of lightly salted water to the boil and add the pak choi. Stir twice, then drain immediately.

5 Place the pak choi in a large bowl, add the dressing and toss to mix. Spoon into a large serving bowl and sprinkle with the crushed peanuts and the stir-fried chilli mixture. Serve warm or cold.

Nutritional information per portion: Energy 79Kcal/329kJ; Protein 1.8g; Carbohydrate 4.5g, of which sugars 4.4g; Fat 6.1g, of which saturates 0.8g; Cholesterol 0mg; Calcium 99mg; Fibre 1.2g; Sodium 398mg.

Steamed vegetables with Chiang Mai spicy dip

In Thailand, steamed vegetables are often partnered with raw ones to create the contrasting textures that are such a feature of the national cuisine. It is a very healthy way to serve them.

SERVES 4

1 head broccoli, divided into florets
130g/4¹/₂oz/1 cup green beans, trimmed
130g/4¹/₂oz asparagus, trimmed
¹/₂ head cauliflower, divided into florets
8 baby corn cobs
130g/4¹/₂oz mangetouts (snow peas)
salt

FOR THE DIP
1 fresh green chilli, seeded
4 garlic cloves, peeled
4 shallots, peeled
2 tomatoes, halved
5 pea aubergines (eggplants)
30ml/2 tbsp lemon juice
30ml/2 tbsp soy sauce
2.5ml/¹/₂ tsp salt
5ml/1 tsp granulated (white) sugar

1 Place the broccoli, green beans, asparagus and cauliflower in a steamer and steam over boiling water for about 4 minutes, until just tender but still with a "bite". Transfer them to a bowl and add the corn cobs and mangetouts. Season to taste with a little salt. Toss to mix, then set aside.

2 Make the dip. Preheat the grill (broiler). Wrap the chilli, garlic, shallots, tomatoes and aubergines in a foil package. Grill (broil) for 10 minutes, until the vegetables have softened, turning the package over once or twice.

3 Unwrap the foil and transfer its contents to a mortar or food processor. Add the lemon juice, soy sauce, salt and sugar. Pound with a pestle or process to a fairly liquid paste.

4 Scrape the dip into a serving bowl or four individual bowls. Serve, surrounded by the steamed and raw vegetables.

Nutritional information per portion: Energy 70Kcal/295kJ; Protein 6.8g; Carbohydrate 8.1g, of which sugars 7.2g; Fat 1.4g, of which saturates 0.3g; Cholesterol 0mg; Calcium 73mg; Fibre 4.7g; Sodium 1005mg.

Stir-fried pineapple with ginger

This dish resembles a fresh mango chutney but with pineapple as the main ingredient. It makes an interesting accompaniment to grilled meat or strongly-flavoured fish such as tuna or swordfish.

SERVES 4

1 pineapple
15ml/1 tbsp vegetable oil
2 garlic cloves, finely chopped
2 shallots, finely chopped
5cm/2in piece fresh root ginger, peeled and finely shredded
30ml/2 tbsp light soy sauce
juice of ¹/₂ lime
1 large fresh red chilli, seeded and finely shredded

1 Trim and peel the pineapple. Cut out the core and dice the flesh.

2 Heat the oil in a wok or frying pan. Stir-fry the garlic and shallots over a medium heat for 2–3 minutes, until golden. Do not let the garlic burn or the dish will taste bitter.

3 Add the pineapple. Stir-fry for about 2 minutes, or until the pineapple cubes start to turn golden on the edges.

4 Add the ginger, soy sauce, lime juice and shredded chilli. Toss together until well mixed. Cook over a low heat for a further 2 minutes, then serve.

Nutritional information per portion: Energy 110Kcal/467kJ; Protein 1g; Carbohydrate 20.8g, of which sugars 20.8g; Fat 3.2g, of which saturates 0.3g; Cholesterol 0mg; Calcium 37mg; Fibre 2.4g; Sodium 538mg.

Rice and noodles

Thai fragrant rice, also known as jasmine rice, is valued for its subtle fragrance, and goes well with both savoury and sweet dishes. In Thailand you are never very far from a noodle seller, and this popular food is bought from breakfast to bedtime. Most noodles are made from rice, though you may also find mung bean noodles.

Savoury fried rice

This is typical Thai street food, eaten at all times of the day. The recipe can be adapted to use whatever vegetables you have available and you could also add meat or shellfish.

SERVES 2

30ml/2 tbsp vegetable oil

2 garlic cloves, finely chopped

1 small fresh red chilli, seeded
    and finely chopped

50g/2oz/1/2 cup cashew nuts, toasted

50g/2oz/2/3 cup desiccated
    (dry unsweetened shredded)
    coconut, toasted

2.5ml/1/2 tsp palm sugar (jaggery) or
    light muscovado (brown) sugar

30ml/2 tbsp light soy sauce

15ml/1 tbsp rice vinegar

1 egg

115g/4oz/1 cup green beans, sliced

1/2 spring cabbage or 115g/4oz spring
    greens (collards) or pak choi
    (bok choy), shredded

90g/31/2oz jasmine rice (raw weight),
    boiled

lime wedges, to serve

1 Heat the oil in a wok or large, heavy frying pan. Add the garlic and cook over a medium to high heat until golden. Do not let the garlic burn or it will taste bitter.

2 Add the red chilli, cashew nuts and toasted coconut to the wok or pan and stir-fry briefly, taking care to prevent the coconut from scorching. Stir in the sugar, soy sauce and rice vinegar. Toss over the heat for 1–2 minutes.

3 Push the stir-fry to one side of the wok or pan and break the egg into the empty side. When the egg is almost set stir it into the garlic and chilli mixture with a wooden spatula or spoon.

4 Add the green beans, greens and cooked rice. Stir over the heat until the greens have just wilted, then spoon into a dish to serve. Offer the lime wedges separately, for squeezing over the rice.

Nutritional information per portion: Energy 548Kcal/2271kJ; Protein 14.6g; Carbohydrate 25.1g, of which sugars 7g; Fat 43.9g, of which saturates 18.2g; Cholesterol 110mg; Calcium 183mg; Fibre 7.5g; Sodium 1200mg.

Festive rice

This pretty Thai dish is traditionally shaped into a cone and surrounded by a variety of accompaniments before being served.

SERVES 8

450g/1lb/2²/₃ cups jasmine rice
60ml/4 tbsp vegetable oil
2 garlic cloves, crushed
2 onions, thinly sliced
2.5ml/¹/₂ tsp ground turmeric
750ml/1¹/₄ pints/3 cups water
400ml/14fl oz/1²/₃ cups coconut milk
1–2 lemon grass stalks, bruised

FOR THE ACCOMPANIMENTS
omelette strips
2 fresh red chillies, seeded
   and shredded
cucumber chunks
tomato wedges
deep-fried onions
prawn (shrimp) crackers

1 Put the jasmine rice in a large strainer and rinse it thoroughly under cold water. Drain well.

2 Heat the oil in a frying pan with a lid. Cook the garlic, onions and turmeric over a low heat for 2–3 minutes, until the onions have softened. Add the rice and stir well to coat in oil.

3 Pour in the water and coconut milk and add the lemon grass. Bring to the boil, stirring. Cover the pan and cook gently for 12 minutes, or until all the liquid has been absorbed by the rice.

4 Remove the pan from the heat and lift the lid. Cover with a clean dish towel, replace the lid and leave to stand in a warm place for 15 minutes. Remove the lemon grass, mound the rice mixture in a cone on a serving platter and garnish with the accompaniments, then serve.

Nutritional information per portion: Energy 285Kcal/1204kJ; Protein 4.6g; Carbohydrate 52.6g, of which sugars 3.8g; Fat 7.7g, of which saturates 0.7g; Cholesterol 0mg; Calcium 49mg; Fibre 0.6g; Sodium 58mg.

Brown rice with lime and lemon grass

It is unusual to find brown rice given the Thai treatment, but the nutty flavour of the grains is enhanced by the fragrance of limes and lemon grass in this delicious dish.

SERVES 4

2 limes

1 lemon grass stalk

225g/8oz/generous 1 cup brown long grain rice

15ml/1 tbsp olive oil

1 onion, chopped

2.5cm/1in piece fresh root ginger, peeled and finely chopped

7.5ml/1½ tsp coriander seeds

7.5ml/1½ tsp cumin seeds

750ml/1¼ pints/3 cups vegetable stock

60ml/4 tbsp chopped fresh coriander (cilantro)

spring onion (scallion) green and toasted coconut strips, to garnish

lime wedges, to serve

1 Pare the limes, using a cannelle knife (zester) or fine grater, and set the rind aside. Finely chop the lower portion of the lemon grass stalk and set aside. Rinse the rice in cold water, put it in a sieve (strainer) and drain thoroughly.

2 Heat the oil in a large pan. Add the onion, ginger, coriander and cumin seeds, lemon grass and lime rind and cook over a low heat for 2–3 minutes.

3 Add the rice to the pan and cook, stirring constantly, for 1 minute, then pour in the stock and bring to the boil. Reduce the heat to very low and cover the pan. Cook gently for 30 minutes, then check the rice. If it is still crunchy, cover the pan and cook for 3–5 minutes more. Remove from the heat.

4 Stir in the fresh coriander, fluff up the rice grains with a fork, cover the pan and leave to stand for 10 minutes. Transfer to a warmed dish, garnish with spring onion green and toasted coconut strips, and serve with lime wedges.

Nutritional information per portion: Energy 241Kcal/1021kJ; Protein 4.4g; Carbohydrate 48.7g, of which sugars 2.7g; Fat 4.6g, of which saturates 0.8g; Cholesterol 0mg; Calcium 15mg; Fibre 1.6g; Sodium 213mg.

Coconut rice

This rich dish is usually served with a tangy papaya salad to balance the sweetness of the coconut milk and sugar. It is one of those comforting treats that everyone enjoys.

SERVES 4

250ml/8fl oz/1 cup water
475ml/16fl oz/2 cups coconut milk
2.5ml/¹/₂ tsp salt
30ml/2 tbsp granulated (white) sugar
450g/1lb/2²/₃ cups jasmine rice

1 Place the water, coconut milk, salt and sugar in a heavy pan. Wash the rice in several changes of cold water until it runs clear.

2 Add the rice to the pan, cover tightly with a lid and bring to the boil over a medium heat. Reduce the heat to low and simmer gently, without lifting the lid unnecessarily, for 15–20 minutes, until the rice is tender and cooked through.

3 Turn off the heat and leave the rice in the pan, still covered with the lid, for a further 5–10 minutes.

4 Gently fluff up the rice with a fork or chopsticks before transferring to a warmed dish and serving.

Nutritional information per portion: Energy 457Kcal/1947kJ; Protein 8.6g; Carbohydrate 102.4g, of which sugars 5.8g; Fat 4.4g, of which saturates 1.3g; Cholesterol 0mg; Calcium 92mg; Fibre 0.5g; Sodium 381mg.

Curried chicken and rice

This simple one-pot meal is perfect for casual entertaining. It can be made using virtually any meat or vegetables that you have to hand.

SERVES 4

60ml/4 tbsp vegetable oil

4 garlic cloves, finely chopped

1 chicken (about 1.5kg/3–3½lb)
   or chicken pieces, skin and bones
   removed and meat cut into
   bitesize pieces

5ml/1 tsp garam masala

450g/1lb/2⅔ cups jasmine rice,
   rinsed and drained

10ml/2 tsp salt

1 litre/1¾ pints/4 cups chicken stock

small bunch fresh coriander (cilantro),
   chopped, to garnish

1 Heat the oil in a wok or large pan that has a lid. Add the garlic and cook over a low to medium heat until golden brown. Add the chicken, increase the heat and brown the pieces on all sides.

2 Add the garam masala, stir well to coat the chicken all over in the spice, then add the drained rice. Add the salt then stir the ingredients together.

3 Pour in the stock, stir well, then cover the wok or pan and bring to the boil. Reduce the heat to low and simmer gently for 10 minutes, until the rice is cooked and tender.

4 Lift the wok or pan off the heat, leaving the lid on, and leave for 10 minutes. Fluff up the rice grains with a fork and spoon on to a platter. Sprinkle with the coriander and serve immediately.

Nutritional information per portion: Energy 719Kcal/3012kJ; Protein 54.9g; Carbohydrate 96.7g, of which sugars 0g; Fat 13.9g, of which saturates 1.9g; Cholesterol 140mg; Calcium 74mg; Fibre 0.5g; Sodium 1360mg.

Thai fried rice

This substantial and tasty dish is based on jasmine rice. Diced chicken, red pepper and corn kernels add colour and extra flavour.

SERVES 4

475ml/16fl oz/2 cups water

50g/2oz/¹⁄₂ cup coconut milk powder

350g/12oz/1³⁄₄ cups jasmine rice, rinsed

30ml/2 tbsp groundnut (peanut) oil

2 garlic cloves, chopped

1 small onion, finely chopped

2.5cm/1in piece of fresh root ginger,
   peeled and grated

225g/8oz skinless, boneless chicken breast
   portions, cut into 1cm/¹⁄₂in dice

1 red (bell) pepper, seeded and sliced

115g/4oz/1 cup drained canned whole
   kernel corn

5ml/1 tsp chilli oil

5ml/1 tsp hot curry powder

2 eggs, beaten

salt

spring onion (scallion) shreds, to garnish

1 Pour the water into a pan and whisk in the coconut milk powder. Add the rice and bring to the boil. Reduce the heat, cover and cook for 12 minutes, or until the rice is tender and the liquid has been absorbed. Spread the rice on a baking sheet and leave until cold.

2 Heat the oil in a wok, add the garlic, onion and ginger and stir-fry over a medium heat for 2 minutes.

3 Push the onion mixture to the sides of the wok, add the chicken to the centre and stir-fry for 2 minutes. Add the rice and toss. Stir-fry over a high heat for about 3 minutes more, until the chicken is cooked through.

4 Stir in the red pepper, corn, chilli oil and curry powder, with salt. Toss over the heat for 1 minute. Stir in the eggs and cook for 1 minute. Garnish with spring onion and serve.

Nutritional information per portion: Energy 573Kcal/2423kJ; Protein 25.4g; Carbohydrate 91.6g, of which sugars 11.2g; Fat 14.2g, of which saturates 2.5g; Cholesterol 154mg; Calcium 102mg; Fibre 1.7g; Sodium 269mg.

Fried rice with pork

This dish is especially easy if you cooked extra rice for a previous meal, but if cooking it freshly, remember to let it cool before frying, otherwise it will not become crisp.

SERVES 4–6

45ml/3 tbsp vegetable oil
1 onion, chopped
15ml/1 tbsp chopped garlic
115g/4oz pork, cut into small cubes
2 eggs, beaten
1kg/2¼lb/4 cups cold cooked rice
30ml/2 tbsp Thai fish sauce
15ml/1 tbsp dark soy sauce
2.5ml/½ tsp caster (superfine) sugar
4 spring onions (scallions),
    finely sliced, to garnish
2 red chillies, sliced, to garnish
1 lime, cut into wedges, to garnish

1 Heat the oil in a wok or large frying pan. Add the onion and garlic and cook for about 2 minutes until softened.

2 Add the pork to the softened onion and garlic. Stir-fry until the pork changes colour and is cooked.

3 Add the eggs and stir-fry until scrambled into small lumps.

4 Add the rice and continue to stir and toss, to coat it with the oil and prevent it from sticking.

5 Add the fish sauce, soy sauce and sugar and mix well. Continue to fry until the rice is thoroughly heated. Spoon into warmed individual bowls and serve, garnished with sliced spring onions, chillies and lime wedges.

Nutritional information per portion: Energy 513Kcal/2165kJ; Protein 17.1g; Carbohydrate 80g, of which sugars 2.1g; Fat 16.1g, of which saturates 2.3g; Cholesterol 132mg; Calcium 75mg; Fibre 0.7g; Sodium 511mg.

Fried rice with beef

One of the joys of Thai cooking is the ease and speed with which a really good meal can be prepared. This one can be on the table in 15 minutes.

SERVES 4

200g/7oz beef steak

15ml/1 tbsp vegetable oil

2 garlic cloves, finely chopped

1 egg

250g/9oz/2¼ cups cooked
   jasmine rice

½ medium head broccoli,
   coarsely chopped

30ml/2 tbsp dark soy sauce

15ml/1 tbsp light soy sauce

5ml/1 tsp palm sugar (jaggery) or
   light muscovado (brown) sugar

15ml/1 tbsp Thai fish sauce

ground black pepper

chilli sauce, to serve

1 Trim the steak and cut into very thin strips with a sharp knife.

2 Heat the oil in a wok or frying pan, add the garlic and cook over a low to medium heat until golden. Do not let it burn. Increase the heat to high, add the steak and stir-fry for 2 minutes.

3 Move the pieces of beef to the edges of the wok or pan and break the egg into the centre. When the egg starts to set, stir-fry it with the meat.

4 Add the rice and toss all the contents of the wok together, scraping up any residue on the base, then add the broccoli, soy sauces, sugar and fish sauce and stir-fry for 2 minutes more. Season to taste with pepper and serve immediately with chilli sauce.

Nutritional information per portion: Energy 250Kcal/1048kJ; Protein 17.9g; Carbohydrate 22.4g, of which sugars 2.8g; Fat 10.4g, of which saturates 3g; Cholesterol 84mg; Calcium 60mg; Fibre 1.7g; Sodium 859mg.

Rice cakes with a prawn and coconut dip

These wonderfully crunchy rice cakes take some time to cook but are very easy to make. The dip is delicious and goes well with other dishes; try it with balls of sticky rice.

SERVES 4–6

150g/5oz/scant 1 cup jasmine rice
400ml/14fl oz/1²/₃ cups boiling water

FOR THE DIP
1 garlic clove, coarsely chopped
small bunch fresh coriander (cilantro),
    coarsely chopped
90g/3¹/₂oz cooked prawns (shrimp),
    peeled and deveined
250ml/8fl oz/1 cup coconut milk
15ml/1 tbsp Thai fish sauce
15ml/1 tbsp light soy sauce
15ml/1 tbsp tamarind juice, made
    by mixing tamarind pulp with
    warm water
5ml/1 tsp palm sugar (jaggery) or
    light muscovado (brown) sugar
30ml/2 tbsp roasted peanuts,
    coarsely chopped
1 fresh red chilli, seeded and chopped

1 Rinse the rice in a sieve (strainer) under running cold water until the water runs clear. Place the rice in a large, heavy pan and pour over the measured boiling water. Stir, bring back to the boil, then reduce the heat and simmer, uncovered, for 15 minutes, or until almost all the water has been absorbed.

2 Reduce the heat to the lowest possible setting – use a heat diffuser if you have one. Cook the rice for a further 2 hours, by which time it should be crisp and stuck to the base of the pan. Continue to cook for a further 5–10 minutes, until the sides of the rice cake begin to come away from the edges of the pan.

3 Preheat the oven to 180°C/350°F/Gas 4. Remove the rice cake by gently easing the tip of a knife under the edges to loosen it all around. Place it on a baking sheet. Bake the rice cake for 20 minutes, until it is golden and crisp, then leave it to cool. Slice it into pieces.

4 To make the dip, place all the ingredients in a food processor and process to a smooth paste. Transfer to a serving bowl and serve with the rice cakes.

Nutritional information per portion: Energy 361Kcal/1508kJ; Protein 11.7g; Carbohydrate 42g, of which sugars 8.8g; Fat 16g, of which saturates 2.9g; Cholesterol 19mg; Calcium 38mg; Fibre 0.8g; Sodium 359mg.

Thai fried noodles

This simple dish, known as Phat Thai, has a fascinating flavour and texture. It is made with rice noodles and is considered one of the national dishes of Thailand.

SERVES 4–6

16 raw tiger prawns (jumbo shrimp)
350g/12oz rice noodles
45ml/3 tbsp vegetable oil
15ml/1 tbsp chopped garlic
2 eggs, lightly beaten
15ml/1 tbsp dried
   shrimp, rinsed
30ml/2 tbsp pickled mooli (daikon)
50g/2oz fried tofu, cut into small slivers
2.5ml/$\frac{1}{2}$ tsp dried chilli flakes
1 large bunch garlic chives, about
   115g/4oz, cut into 5cm/2in lengths

225g/8oz/2$\frac{1}{2}$ cups beansprouts
50g/2oz/$\frac{1}{2}$ cup roasted peanuts,
   coarsely ground
5ml/1 tsp granulated (white) sugar
15ml/1 tbsp dark soy sauce
30ml/2 tbsp Thai fish sauce
30ml/2 tbsp tamarind juice, made
   by mixing tamarind paste with
   warm water
fresh coriander (cilantro) leaves and lime
   wedges, to garnish

1 Peel the prawns, leaving the tails intact. Carefully cut along the back of each prawn and remove the dark vein.

2 Place the rice noodles in a large bowl, add warm water to cover and leave to soak for 20–30 minutes, then drain thoroughly and set aside.

3 Heat 15ml/1 tbsp of the oil in a wok. Stir-fry the garlic until golden. Stir in the prawns and cook for 1–2 minutes, until pink. Remove and set aside.

4 Heat 15ml/1 tbsp of the remaining oil in the wok. Add the eggs and tilt the wok to make a thin layer. Stir to scramble and break up. Remove from the wok and set aside with the prawns.

5 Heat the remaining oil in the same wok. Add the dried shrimp, pickled mooli, tofu slivers and dried chilli flakes. Stir briefly. Add the noodles and stir-fry for about 5 minutes.

6 Add the garlic chives, half the beansprouts and half the ground roasted peanuts to the wok. Stir briefly.

7 Add the granulated sugar, soy sauce, fish sauce and tamarind juice. Mix all the ingredients together well and cook until the noodles are heated through.

8 Return the prawn and egg mixture to the wok and mix with the noodles. Serve topped with the remaining beansprouts and peanuts, and garnished with the coriander leaves and lime wedges.

Nutritional information per portion: Energy 580Kcal/2416kJ; Protein 21.2g; Carbohydrate 76g, of which sugars 2.7g; Fat 20g, of which saturates 3.1g; Cholesterol 169mg; Calcium 256mg; Fibre 1.6g; Sodium 647mg.

Plain noodles with four flavours

A wonderfully simple way of serving noodles, this dish allows each individual diner to season their own, sprinkling over the four flavours as they like.

SERVES 4

4 small fresh red or green chillies
60ml/4 tbsp Thai fish sauce
60ml/4 tbsp rice vinegar
granulated (white) sugar
mild or hot chilli powder
350g/12oz fresh or dried noodles

1 Prepare the four flavours. For the first, finely chop 2 small red or green chillies, discarding the seeds. Or, if you prefer, leave the seeds in for extra heat. Place them in a small bowl and add the Thai fish sauce.

2 For the second flavour, chop the remaining chillies finely and mix them with the rice vinegar in a small bowl. Put the sugar and chilli powder in separate small bowls.

3 Cook the noodles until tender, following the instructions on the packet. Drain well, transfer to a large bowl and serve immediately with the four flavours handed separately.

Nutritional information per portion: Energy 55Kcal/236kJ; Protein 2g; Carbohydrate 11.6g, of which sugars 0.4g; Fat 0.5g, of which saturates 0.1g; Cholesterol 5mg; Calcium 5mg; Fibre 0.5g; Sodium 191mg.

Thai noodles with garlic chives

This recipe requires a little time for preparation, but the cooking time is very fast. Everything is cooked in one pot and should be eaten immediately. This is a filling and tasty vegetarian dish.

SERVES 4

350g/12oz dried rice noodles

1cm/½in piece fresh root ginger, peeled and grated

30ml/2 tbsp light soy sauce

45ml/3 tbsp vegetable oil

225g/8oz Quorn (mycoprotein), cut into small cubes

2 garlic cloves, crushed

1 large onion, cut into thin wedges

115g/4oz fried tofu, thinly sliced

1 green chilli, seeded and thinly sliced

175g/6oz/2 cups beansprouts

2 large bunches garlic chives, about 115g/4oz, cut into 5cm/2in lengths

50g/2oz/½ cup roasted peanuts, ground

30ml/2 tbsp dark soy sauce

30ml/2 tbsp chopped fresh coriander (cilantro), and 1 lemon, cut into wedges, to garnish

1 Place the noodles in a bowl, cover with warm water and leave to soak for 30 minutes. Drain and set aside.

2 Mix the ginger, light soy sauce and 15ml/1 tbsp of the oil in a bowl. Add the Quorn. Set aside for 10 minutes. Drain, reserving the marinade.

3 Heat 15ml/1 tbsp of the oil in a frying pan and cook the garlic for a few seconds. Add the Quorn and stir-fry for 3–4 minutes, then set aside on a plate.

4 Heat the remaining oil in the pan. Stir-fry the onion for 3–4 minutes, until softened. Add the tofu and chilli, stir-fry briefly and add the noodles. Cook over a medium heat for 4–5 minutes.

5 Stir in the beansprouts, garlic chives and most of the ground peanuts. Stir well, then add the Quorn, the dark soy sauce and the reserved marinade.

6 Serve garnished with the rest of the peanuts, coriander and lemon.

Nutritional information per portion: Energy 551Kcal/2299kJ; Protein 23.3g; Carbohydrate 82.3g, of which sugars 7.1g; Fat 13.1g, of which saturates 1.5g; Cholesterol 0mg; Calcium 470mg; Fibre 5g; Sodium 1221mg.

Special chow mein

Another example of the Chinese influence in Thai cooking. Lap cheong is a special air-dried Chinese sausage and is available from most Chinese supermarkets.

SERVES 4–6

450g/1lb egg noodles
45ml/3 tbsp vegetable oil
2 garlic cloves, sliced
5ml/1 tsp chopped fresh root ginger
2 fresh red chillies, seeded and chopped
2 lap cheong, total weight about
   75g/3oz, rinsed and sliced (optional)
1 skinless, boneless chicken breast
   portion, thinly sliced
16 raw tiger prawns (jumbo shrimp),
   peeled, tails left intact, and deveined

115g/4oz/2 cups green beans
225g/8oz/2¹/₂ cups beansprouts
small bunch garlic chives, about 50g/2oz
30ml/2 tbsp soy sauce
15ml/1 tbsp oyster sauce
15ml/1 tbsp sesame oil
salt and ground black pepper
2 shredded spring onions (scallions) and
   fresh coriander (cilantro) leaves, to
   garnish

1 Cook the noodles in a large pan of boiling water, according to the instructions on the packet. When they are cooked, drain them well and set aside.

2 Heat 15ml/1 tbsp of the oil in a wok or large frying pan and stir-fry the garlic, ginger and chillies for 2 minutes. Take care not to burn the garlic. Add the lap cheong, if using, chicken, prawns and beans. Stir-fry over a high heat for 2 minutes more, or until the chicken and prawns are cooked. Transfer the mixture to a bowl and set aside.

3 Heat the rest of the oil in the wok. Add the beansprouts and garlic chives and stir-fry for 1–2 minutes. Add the drained noodles and toss over the heat to mix. Season with the soy sauce, oyster sauce and salt and pepper to taste. Return the prawn mixture to the wok. Mix well with the noodles and toss until heated through.

4 Stir the sesame oil into the noodles. Spoon into a warmed bowl and serve immediately, garnished with the spring onions and coriander leaves.

Nutritional information per portion: Energy 624Kcal/2631kJ; Protein 29.3g; Carbohydrate 84.5g, of which sugars 4.6g; Fat 21.2g, of which saturates 4.2g; Cholesterol 107mg; Calcium 76mg; Fibre 4.8g; Sodium 808mg.

Mee krob

The name of this dish means "deep-fried noodles" and it is very popular in Thailand. The taste is a stunning combination of sweet and hot, salty and sour, while the texture contrives to be both crisp and chewy.

SERVES 1

vegetable oil, for deep-frying
130g/4¹/₂oz rice vermicelli noodles

juice of 1 lime
2.5ml/¹/₂ tsp dried chilli flakes

FOR THE SAUCE
30ml/2 tbsp vegetable oil
130g/4¹/₂oz fried tofu,
    cut into thin strips
2 garlic cloves, finely chopped
2 small shallots, finely chopped
15ml/1 tbsp light soy sauce
30ml/2 tbsp palm sugar (jaggery) or
    light muscovado (brown) sugar
60ml/4 tbsp vegetable stock

FOR THE GARNISH
15ml/1 tbsp vegetable oil
1 egg, lightly beaten with
    15ml/1 tbsp cold water
25g/1oz/¹/₃ cup beansprouts
1 spring onion (scallion), thinly shredded
1 red chilli, seeded and finely chopped
1 whole head pickled garlic, sliced across
    the bulb

1 Heat the oil for deep-frying in a wok or large pan to 190°C/375°F or until a cube of bread, added to the oil, browns in about 45 seconds. Add the noodles and deep-fry until golden and crisp. Drain on kitchen paper and set aside.

2 Make the sauce. Heat the oil in a wok, add the fried tofu and cook over a medium heat until crisp. Using a slotted spoon, transfer it to a plate.

3 Add the garlic and shallots to the wok and cook until golden brown. Stir in the soy sauce, sugar, stock, lime juice and chilli flakes. Cook, stirring, until the mixture begins to caramelize. Add the reserved tofu and stir until it has soaked up some of the liquid. Remove the wok from the heat and set aside.

4 Prepare the egg garnish. Heat the oil in a wok or frying pan. Pour in the egg in a thin stream to form trails. As soon as it sets, lift out and place on a plate.

5 Crumble the noodles into the sauce, mix well, then spoon into warmed bowls. Sprinkle with rest of the garnish ingredients and serve immediately.

Nutritional information per portion: Energy 1293Kcal/5362kJ; Protein 28.8g; Carbohydrate 109.1g, of which sugars 2g; Fat 80.5g, of which saturates 10.6g; Cholesterol 509mg; Calcium 733mg; Fibre 0.4g; Sodium 1180mg.

Spicy fried noodles

This is a wonderfully versatile dish as you can adapt it to include your favourite ingredients – just as long as you keep a balance of flavours, textures and colours.

SERVES 4

225g/8oz egg thread noodles
60ml/4 tbsp vegetable oil
2 garlic cloves, finely chopped
175g/6oz pork fillet (tenderloin), sliced into thin strips
1 skinless, boneless chicken breast (about 175g/6oz), sliced into thin strips
115g/4oz/1 cup cooked peeled prawns (shrimp), rinsed if canned
45ml/3 tbsp fresh lemon juice
45ml/3 tbsp Thai fish sauce
30ml/2 tbsp soft light brown sugar
2 eggs, beaten
1/2 red chilli, seeded and finely chopped
50g/2oz/2/3 cup beansprouts
60ml/4 tbsp roasted peanuts, chopped
3 spring onions (scallions), cut into 5cm/2in lengths and shredded
45ml/3 tbsp chopped fresh coriander (cilantro)

1 Bring a large pan of water to the boil. Add the noodles, remove the pan from the heat and leave for 5 minutes.

2 Meanwhile, heat 45ml/3 tbsp of the oil in a wok or large frying pan, add the garlic and cook for 30 seconds. Add the pork and chicken and stir-fry until browned, then add the prawns and stir-fry for 2 minutes. Stir in the lemon juice, then add the fish sauce and sugar. Stir-fry until the sugar has dissolved.

3 Drain the noodles and add to the wok or pan with the remaining 15ml/ 1 tbsp oil. Toss all the ingredients together. Pour the beaten eggs over the noodles and stir-fry until almost set, then add the chilli and beansprouts.

4 Divide the peanuts, spring onions and coriander into two portions. Add one portion to the pan and stir-fry for 2 minutes. Transfer the noodles to a platter. Sprinkle on the remaining peanuts, spring onions and coriander and serve.

Nutritional information per portion: Energy 570Kcal/2391kJ; Protein 38.5g; Carbohydrate 48.9g, of which sugars 8.7g; Fat 25.9g, of which saturates 5.1g; Cholesterol 241mg; Calcium 73mg; Fibre 2.5g; Sodium 700mg.

Southern curried noodles

Chicken or pork can be used to provide the protein in this tasty dish. It is so quick and easy to prepare and cook, it makes the perfect snack for busy people.

SERVES 2

30ml/2 tbsp vegetable oil

10ml/2 tsp magic paste

1 lemon grass stalk, finely chopped

5ml/1 tsp Thai red curry paste

90g/3½oz skinless, boneless chicken
    breast or pork fillet (tenderloin),
    sliced into slivers

30ml/2 tbsp light soy sauce

400ml/14fl oz/1⅔ cups coconut milk

2 kaffir lime leaves, rolled into cylinders
    and thinly sliced

250g/9oz dried medium egg noodles

90g/3½oz Chinese leaves (Chinese
    cabbage), shredded

90g/3½oz spinach or watercress
    (leaves), shredded

juice of 1 lime

small bunch fresh coriander
    (cilantro), chopped

1 Heat the oil in a wok or large, heavy frying pan. Add the magic paste and lemon grass and stir-fry over a low to medium heat for 4–5 seconds, until they give off their aroma.

2 Stir in the curry paste, then add the chicken or pork. Stir-fry over a medium to high heat for 2 minutes, until the meat is coated in the paste and seared on all sides.

3 Add the soy sauce, coconut milk and sliced lime leaves. Bring to a simmer, then add the noodles.

4 Simmer gently for 4 minutes, tossing the mixture occasionally to make sure that the noodles cook evenly.

5 Add the Chinese leaves and spinach or watercress. Stir in the lime juice. Spoon into a warmed bowl, sprinkle with the coriander and serve.

Nutritional information per portion: Energy 709Kcal/2989kJ; Protein 29.5g; Carbohydrate 102.1g, of which sugars 14.6g; Fat 23.1g, of which saturates 4.8g; Cholesterol 69mg; Calcium 251mg; Fibre 5.5g; Sodium 1666mg.

Chiang Mai noodles

An interesting noodle dish that combines soft, boiled noodles with crisp deep-fried ones and adds the usual panoply of Thai sweet, hot and sour flavours.

SERVES 4

250ml/8fl oz/1 cup coconut cream
15ml/1 tbsp magic paste
5ml/1 tsp Thai red curry paste
450g/1lb chicken thigh meat, chopped
    into small pieces
30ml/2 tbsp dark soy sauce
2 red (bell) peppers, diced
600ml/1 pint/2$^{1}/_{2}$ cups chicken or
    vegetable stock
90g/3$^{1}/_{2}$oz fresh or dried rice noodles

FOR THE GARNISHES
vegetable oil, for deep-frying
90g/3$^{1}/_{2}$oz fine dried rice noodles
2 pickled garlic cloves, chopped
small bunch coriander (cilantro), chopped
2 limes, cut into wedges

1 Pour the coconut cream into a large wok or frying pan and bring to the boil over a medium heat. Continue to boil, stirring frequently, for 8–10 minutes, until the milk separates and an oily sheen appears on the surface.

2 Add the magic paste and red curry paste and cook, stirring constantly, for 3–5 seconds, until they give off a fragrant aroma.

3 Add the chicken and toss over the heat until sealed on all sides. Stir in the soy sauce and the diced peppers and stir-fry for 3–4 minutes. Pour in the stock. Bring to the boil, then lower the heat and simmer for 10–15 minutes, until the chicken is fully cooked.

4 Meanwhile, make the noodle garnish. Heat the oil in a pan or deep-fryer to 190°C/375°F or until a cube of bread, added to the oil, browns in 45 seconds. Break all the noodles in half, then divide them into four portions. Add one portion at a time to the hot oil. They will puff up on contact. As soon as they are crisp, lift the noodles out with a slotted spoon and drain on kitchen paper.

5 Bring a large pan of water to the boil and cook the noodles until tender, following the instructions on the packet. Drain well, divide among four dishes, then spoon the curry sauce over them. Top each portion with a cluster of fried noodles. Sprinkle the pickled garlic and coriander over the top and serve immediately with lime wedges.

Nutritional information per portion: Energy 360Kcal/1501kJ; Protein 26.8g; Carbohydrate 25.4g, of which sugars 6.7g; Fat 16.6g, of which saturates 12.1g; Cholesterol 118mg; Calcium 22mg; Fibre 1.4g; Sodium 281mg.

Thai crispy noodles with beef

Rice vermicelli is deep-fried before being added to this dish, and in the process the vermicelli expands to at least four times its original size.

SERVES 4

450g/1lb rump (round) steak
teriyaki sauce, for brushing
175g/6oz rice vermicelli
groundnut (peanut) oil, for deep-frying
    and stir-frying
8 spring onions (scallions),
    diagonally sliced
2 garlic cloves, crushed
4–5 carrots, cut into julienne strips

1–2 fresh red chillies, seeded
    and finely sliced
2 small courgettes (zucchini),
    diagonally sliced
5ml/1 tsp grated fresh root ginger
60ml/4 tbsp rice vinegar
90ml/6 tbsp light soy sauce
about 475ml/16fl oz/2 cups spicy stock

1 Beat the steak to about 2.5cm/1in thick. Place in a shallow dish, brush with the teriyaki sauce and set aside for 2–4 hours to marinate.

2 Separate the rice vermicelli into manageable loops. Pour oil into a wok to a depth of about 5cm/2in, and heat until a strand of vermicelli cooks when lowered into the oil.

3 Carefully add a loop of vermicelli to the oil. Almost immediately, turn to cook on the other side, then remove and drain on kitchen paper. Repeat with the remaining loops. Transfer the noodles to a separate wok or bowl and keep warm while you cook the steak and vegetables.

4 Strain the oil from the wok into a heatproof bowl and set aside. Heat 15ml/1 tbsp groundnut oil in the clean wok. Fry the steak for about 30 seconds on each side, until browned. Transfer to a board and cut into thick slices. The meat should be browned on the outside but still pink inside. Set aside.

5 Add a little extra oil to the wok, add the spring onions, garlic and carrots and stir-fry over a medium heat for 5–6 minutes, until the carrots are slightly soft and glazed. Add the chillies, courgettes and ginger and stir-fry for 1–2 minutes.

6 Stir in the rice vinegar, soy sauce and stock. Cook for 4 minutes, or until the sauce has thickened slightly. Return the steak to the wok and cook for a further 1–2 minutes. Spoon the steak, vegetables and sauce over the noodles and toss lightly. Serve immediately.

Nutritional information per portion: Energy 493Kcal/2052kJ; Protein 29.5g; Carbohydrate 43.4g, of which sugars 7.2g; Fat 21.9g, of which saturates 5.7g; Cholesterol 65mg; Calcium 43mg; Fibre 2g; Sodium 1697mg.

Salads

This chapter contains a selection of salads, big and small, made from fresh and cooked vegetables, often with a little chicken, beef or seafood added. In Thailand, salads can be a meal in themselves or just one of several dishes that are brought to the table as and when they are ready.

Raw vegetable yam

In this context, the word "yam" does not refer to the starchy vegetable that resembles sweet potato, but rather to a unique style of Thai cooking. Yam dishes are salads made with raw or lightly cooked vegetables, dressed with a special spicy sauce.

SERVES 4

50g/2oz watercress or baby spinach, chopped
1/2 cucumber, finely diced
2 celery sticks, finely diced
2 carrots, finely diced
1 red (bell) pepper, seeded and finely diced
2 tomatoes, seeded and finely diced
small bunch fresh mint, chopped
90g/3½oz cellophane noodles

FOR THE YAM

2 small fresh red chillies, seeded and
    finely chopped
60ml/4 tbsp light soy sauce

45ml/3 tbsp lemon juice
5ml/1 tsp palm sugar (jaggery) or
    light muscovado (brown) sugar
60ml/4 tbsp water
1 head pickled garlic, finely chopped,
    plus 15ml/1 tbsp vinegar from the jar
50g/2oz/scant ½ cup peanuts, roasted
    and chopped
90g/3½oz fried tofu, finely chopped
15ml/1 tbsp sesame seeds, toasted

1 Place the watercress or spinach, cucumber, celery, carrots, red pepper and tomatoes in a bowl. Add the chopped mint and toss together.

2 Soak the noodles in boiling water for 3 minutes, or according to the packet instructions, then drain well and snip with scissors into shorter lengths. Add them to the vegetables.

3 Make the yam. Put the chopped chillies in a pan and add the soy sauce, lemon juice, sugar and water. Place over a medium heat and stir until the sugar has dissolved.

4 Add the garlic to the pan, with the pickling vinegar from the jar, then mix in the chopped peanuts, tofu and toasted sesame seeds.

5 Pour the yam over the vegetables and noodles, toss together until well mixed, and serve immediately.

Nutritional information per portion: Energy 490Kcal/2043kJ; Protein 18.9g; Carbohydrate 28.5g, of which sugars 21g; Fat 34.3g, of which saturates 8.6g; Cholesterol 0mg; Calcium 80mg; Fibre 6.2g; Sodium 493mg.

Southern-style yam

The food of the southern region is notoriously hot and because of the proximity to the borders with Malaysia, Thailand's Muslim minority are mostly to be found in this area.

SERVES FOUR

90g/3¹/₂oz Chinese leaves (Chinese cabbage), shredded
90g/3¹/₂oz/generous 1 cup beansprouts
90g/3¹/₂oz/scant 1 cup green beans, trimmed
90g/3¹/₂oz broccoli, preferably purple sprouting, divided into florets
15ml/1 tbsp sesame seeds, toasted

FOR THE YAM

60ml/4 tbsp coconut cream
5ml/1 tsp Thai red curry paste
90g/3¹/₂oz/1¹/₄ cups oyster mushrooms or field (portabello) mushrooms, sliced
60ml/4 tbsp coconut milk
5ml/1 tsp ground turmeric
5ml/1 tsp thick tamarind juice, made by mixing tamarind paste with warm water
juice of ¹/₂ lemon
60ml/4 tbsp light soy sauce
5ml/1 tsp palm sugar (jaggery) or light muscovado (brown) sugar

1 Steam the shredded Chinese leaves, beansprouts, green beans and broccoli separately or blanch them in boiling water for 1 minute per batch. Drain, place in a serving bowl and leave to cool.

2 Make the yam. Pour the coconut cream into a wok or large frying pan and heat gently for 2–3 minutes, until it separates. Stir in the red curry paste. Cook over a low heat for 30 seconds, until the mixture is fragrant.

3 Increase the heat to high and add the mushrooms to the wok or pan. Cook for a further 2–3 minutes.

4 Pour in the coconut milk and add the ground turmeric, tamarind juice, lemon juice, soy sauce and sugar to the wok or pan. Mix thoroughly.

5 Pour the coconut mixture over the prepared vegetables and toss well to combine. Sprinkle with the toasted sesame seeds and serve immediately.

Nutritional information per portion: Energy 89Kcal/368kJ; Protein 4.2g; Carbohydrate 4.1g, of which sugars 3.4g; Fat 6.3g, of which saturates 3.4g; Cholesterol 0mg; Calcium 90mg; Fibre 2g; Sodium 1122mg.

Green papaya salad

This salad appears in many guises in South-east Asia. As green papaya is not easy to get hold of, finely grated carrots, cucumber or even crisp green apple can be used instead.

SERVES 4

1 green papaya
4 garlic cloves, coarsely chopped
15ml/1 tbsp chopped shallots
3–4 fresh red chillies, seeded
   and sliced
2.5ml/½ tsp salt
2–3 snake beans or 6 green beans, cut
   into 2cm/¾in lengths
2 tomatoes, cut into thin wedges
45ml/3 tbsp Thai fish sauce
15ml/1 tbsp caster (superfine) sugar
juice of 1 lime
30ml/2 tbsp crushed roasted peanuts
sliced fresh red chillies, to garnish

1 Cut the papaya in half lengthways. Scrape out the seeds with a spoon and discard, then peel, using a swivel vegetable peeler or a small sharp knife. Shred the flesh finely in a food processor or using a grater.

2 Put the garlic, shallots, red chillies and salt in a large mortar and grind to a paste with a pestle. Add the shredded papaya, a small amount at a time, pounding with the pestle until it becomes slightly limp and soft.

3 Add the sliced snake or green beans and wedges of tomato to the mortar and crush them lightly with the pestle until they are incorporated.

4 Add the mixture with the fish sauce, sugar and lime juice and mix well. Transfer the salad to a serving dish and sprinkle with the crushed roasted peanuts. Garnish with the sliced red chillies and serve the salad immediately.

Nutritional information per portion: Energy 63Kcal/263kJ; Protein 2.5g; Carbohydrate 6.2g, of which sugars 5.6g; Fat 3.3g, of which saturates 0.6g; Cholesterol 0mg; Calcium 19mg; Fibre 1.8g; Sodium 835mg.

Hot and sour noodle salad

Noodles make the perfect basis for a salad, absorbing the dressing and providing a contrast in texture to the crisp vegetables.

SERVES 2

200g/7oz thin rice noodles
small bunch fresh coriander (cilantro)
2 tomatoes, seeded and sliced
130g/4¹/₂oz baby corn cobs, sliced
4 spring onions (scallions), thinly sliced
1 red (bell) pepper, seeded and chopped
juice of 2 limes
2 small fresh green chillies, seeded and chopped
10ml/2 tsp granulated (white) sugar
115g/4oz/1 cup peanuts, toasted and chopped
30ml/2 tbsp soy sauce
salt

1 Bring a pan of lightly salted water to the boil. Snap the noodles into short lengths, add to the pan and cook for 3–4 minutes. Drain, rinse under cold water and drain again.

2 Set aside a few coriander leaves for the garnish. Chop the remaining leaves and place them in a large serving bowl.

3 Add the noodles to the bowl, with the tomato slices, corn cobs, spring onions, red pepper, lime juice, chillies, sugar and chopped peanuts. Season with the soy sauce, then taste and add a little salt if you think the mixture needs it. Toss the salad lightly but thoroughly, then garnish with the reserved coriander leaves and serve immediately.

Nutritional information per portion: Energy 761Kcal/3173kJ; Protein 24.1g; Carbohydrate 101.6g, of which sugars 15.6g; Fat 27.7g, of which saturates 5.2g; Cholesterol 0mg; Calcium 117mg; Fibre 7.9g; Sodium 1840mg.

Fried egg salad

Chillies and eggs may seem unlikely partners, but work very well together. The peppery taste of the watercress makes it ideal for this salad, but you could also use rocket (arugula).

SERVES 2

15ml/1 tbsp groundnut (peanut) oil
1 garlic clove, thinly sliced
4 eggs
2 shallots, thinly sliced
2 small fresh red chillies, seeded and
   thinly sliced
½ small cucumber, finely diced
1cm/½in piece fresh root ginger,
   peeled and grated
juice of 2 limes
30ml/2 tbsp soy sauce
5ml/1 tsp caster (superfine) sugar
small bunch coriander (cilantro)
bunch watercress, coarsely chopped

1 Heat the oil in a frying pan. Add the garlic and cook over a low heat until it starts to turn golden. Crack in the eggs. Break the yolks with a wooden spatula, then fry until the eggs are almost firm. Remove from the pan and set aside.

2 Mix the shallots, chillies, cucumber and ginger in a bowl. In a separate bowl, whisk the lime juice with the soy sauce and sugar, pour over the vegetables and toss lightly.

3 Set aside a few of the coriander sprigs for the garnish. Chop the rest and add them to the salad. Toss it again.

4 Reserve a few watercress sprigs for the garnish and arrange the rest on two serving plates. Cut the eggs into slices and divide between the watercress mounds. Spoon the shallot mixture over and serve, garnished with coriander and watercress sprigs.

Nutritional information per portion: Energy 215Kcal/894kJ; Protein 14.2g; Carbohydrate 2.4g, of which sugars 2.2g; Fat 16.9g, of which saturates 4.2g; Cholesterol 381mg; Calcium 112mg; Fibre 0.8g; Sodium 1223mg.

Thai fruit and vegetable salad

This fruit salad is traditionally presented with the main course and serves as a cooler to counteract the heat of the chillies that will inevitably be present in the other dishes. It is a typically harmonious balance of flavours.

SERVES 4–6

1 small pineapple

1 small mango, peeled and sliced

1 green apple, cored and sliced

6 rambutans or lychees, peeled
  and stoned (pitted)

115g/4oz/1 cup green beans, trimmed and halved

1 red onion, sliced

1 small cucumber, cut into short sticks

115g/4oz/1⅓ cups beansprouts

2 spring onions (scallions), sliced

1 ripe tomato, quartered

225g/8oz cos, romaine or iceberg lettuce leaves

FOR THE COCONUT DIPPING SAUCE

30ml/2 tbsp coconut cream

30ml/2 tbsp granulated (white) sugar

75ml/5 tbsp boiling water

1.5ml/¼ tsp chilli sauce

15ml/1 tbsp Thai fish sauce

juice of 1 lime

1 Make the coconut dipping sauce. Spoon the coconut cream, sugar and boiling water into a screw-top jar. Add the chilli and fish sauces and lime juice, close tightly and shake to mix.

2 Trim both ends of the pineapple with a knife, then cut away the skin. Remove the central core with an apple corer. Alternatively, quarter the pineapple lengthways and remove the portion of core from each wedge with a knife. Chop the pineapple and set aside with the other fruits.

3 Bring a small pan of lightly salted water to the boil over a medium heat. Add the green beans and cook for 3–4 minutes, until just tender but still retaining some "bite". Drain, refresh under cold running water, drain well again and set aside.

4 To serve, arrange all the fruits and vegetables in small heaps on a platter or in a shallow bowl. Pour the coconut sauce into a small serving bowl and serve separately as a dip.

Nutritional information per portion: Energy 159Kcal/673kJ; Protein 3.5g; Carbohydrate 32.2g, of which sugars 31g; Fat 2.7g, of which saturates 1.7g; Cholesterol 0mg; Calcium 69mg; Fibre 4.7g; Sodium 188mg.

Bamboo shoot salad

This hot, sharp-flavoured salad originated in north-eastern Thailand. Use canned whole bamboo shoots, if you can find them – they have more flavour than sliced ones.

SERVES 4

400g/14oz canned bamboo shoots,
   cut in large pieces
25g/1oz/about 3 tbsp glutinous rice
30ml/2 tbsp chopped shallots
15ml/1 tbsp chopped garlic
45ml/3 tbsp chopped spring
   onions (scallions)
30ml/2 tbsp Thai fish sauce
30ml/2 tbsp fresh lime juice
5ml/1 tsp granulated (white) sugar
2.5ml/½ tsp dried chilli flakes
20–25 small fresh mint leaves
15ml/1 tbsp toasted sesame seeds

1 Rinse the bamboo shoots under cold running water, then drain them, pat them thoroughly dry with kitchen paper and set them aside.

2 Dry-roast the rice in a frying pan until golden brown. Leave to cool slightly, then place in a mortar and grind to fine crumbs with a pestle.

3 Transfer the rice to a bowl and add the shallots, garlic, spring onions, fish sauce, lime juice, sugar, chillies and half the mint leaves. Mix well.

4 Add the bamboo shoots to the bowl and toss to mix. Serve sprinkled with toasted sesame seeds and the remaining mint leaves.

Nutritional information per portion: Energy 80Kcal/336kJ; Protein 4.5g; Carbohydrate 9.4g, of which sugars 2.9g; Fat 2.8g, of which saturates 0.4g; Cholesterol 0mg; Calcium 51mg; Fibre 2g; Sodium 185mg.

Cabbage salad

This is a simple and delicious way of serving a somewhat mundane vegetable. Classic Thai flavours permeate this colourful warm salad.

SERVES 4–6

30ml/2 tbsp vegetable oil

2 large fresh red chillies, seeded and cut into thin strips

6 garlic cloves, thinly sliced

6 shallots, thinly sliced

1 small cabbage, shredded

30ml/2 tbsp coarsely chopped roasted peanuts, to garnish

FOR THE DRESSING

30ml/2 tbsp Thai fish sauce

grated rind of 1 lime

30ml/2 tbsp fresh lime juice

120ml/4fl oz/½ cup coconut milk

1 Make the dressing by mixing the fish sauce, lime rind and juice and coconut milk in a bowl. Whisk until thoroughly combined. Set aside.

2 Heat the oil in a wok. Stir-fry the chillies, garlic and shallots over a medium heat for 3–4 minutes, until the shallots are brown and crisp. Remove from the wok with a slotted spoon and set aside.

3 Bring a large pan of lightly salted water to the boil. Add the cabbage and blanch for 2–3 minutes. Drain it well in a sieve (strainer) or colander, then transfer to a bowl.

4 Whisk the dressing again, add to the warm cabbage and toss to mix. Transfer to a serving dish. Sprinkle with the fried shallot mixture and the peanuts. Serve immediately.

Nutritional information per portion: Energy 124Kcal/513kJ; Protein 3.4g; Carbohydrate 7.1g, of which sugars 6.5g; Fat 9.2g, of which saturates 1.4g; Cholesterol 0mg; Calcium 57mg; Fibre 2.3g; Sodium 306mg.

Seafood salad with fragrant herbs

This is a spectacular salad made with cellophane noodles. The luscious combination of prawns, scallops and squid makes it the ideal choice for a special celebration.

SERVES 4–6

250ml/8fl oz/1 cup fish stock or water

350g/12oz squid, cleaned and cut into rings

12 raw king prawns (jumbo shrimp), peeled, with tails intact

12 scallops

50g/2oz cellophane noodles, soaked in warm water for 30 minutes

½ cucumber, cut into thin batons

1 lemon grass stalk, finely chopped

2 kaffir lime leaves, finely shredded

2 shallots, thinly sliced

30ml/2 tbsp chopped spring onions (scallions)

30ml/2 tbsp fresh coriander (cilantro) leaves

12–15 fresh mint leaves, coarsely torn

4 fresh red chillies, seeded and cut into slivers

juice of 1–2 limes

30ml/2 tbsp Thai fish sauce

fresh coriander sprigs, to garnish

1 Pour the fish stock or water into a medium pan, set over a high heat and bring to the boil. Cook each type of seafood separately in the stock for 3–4 minutes. Remove with a slotted spoon and set aside to cool.

2 Drain the noodles. Using scissors, cut them into short lengths, about 5cm/2in long. Place them in a serving bowl and add the cucumber, lemon grass, kaffir lime leaves, shallots, spring onions, coriander, mint and chillies.

3 Pour over the lime juice and fish sauce. Mix well, then add the seafood. Toss lightly. Garnish with the fresh coriander sprigs and serve.

Nutritional information per portion: Energy 135Kcal/568kJ; Protein 22.3g; Carbohydrate 4.6g, of which sugars 4.3g; Fat 3.1g, of which saturates 0.5g; Cholesterol 100mg; Calcium 173mg; Fibre 1.5g; Sodium 359mg.

Pomelo salad

Typically, a Thai meal includes a selection of about five dishes, one of which is often a refreshing and palate-cleansing salad that features tropical fruit.

SERVES 4–6

30ml/2 tbsp vegetable oil
4 shallots, finely sliced
2 garlic cloves, finely sliced
1 large pomelo
15ml/1 tbsp roasted peanuts
115g/4oz cooked peeled prawns (shrimp)
115g/4oz cooked crab meat
10–12 small fresh mint leaves

FOR THE DRESSING

30ml/2 tbsp Thai fish sauce
15ml/1 tbsp palm sugar (jaggery) or
    light muscovado (brown) sugar
30ml/2 tbsp fresh lime juice

FOR THE GARNISH

2 spring onions (scallions), thinly sliced
2 fresh red chillies, seeded and thinly sliced
fresh coriander (cilantro) leaves
shredded fresh coconut (optional)

1 To make the dressing, mix the fish sauce, sugar and lime juice together. Whisk well, then cover with clear film (plastic wrap) and set aside.

2 Heat the oil in a small frying pan, add the shallots and garlic and cook over a medium heat until they are golden. Remove from the pan and set aside.

3 Peel the pomelo and break into small pieces, removing membranes.

4 Grind the peanuts coarsely and put in a bowl. Add the pomelo, prawns, crab meat, mint and shallot mixture. Pour over the dressing, toss and sprinkle with the spring onions, chillies and coriander and shredded coconut, if using. Serve immediately.

Nutritional information per portion: Energy 159Kcal/665kJ; Protein 13.4g; Carbohydrate 8.4g, of which sugars 8.1g; Fat 8.2g, of which saturates 1.1g; Cholesterol 44mg; Calcium 107mg; Fibre 1.1g; Sodium 1004mg.

Aubergine salad with shrimp and egg

This is an appetizing and unusual salad that you will find yourself making over and over again. Roasting the aubergines really brings out their flavour.

SERVES 4–6

2 aubergines (eggplants)
15ml/1 tbsp vegetable oil
30ml/2 tbsp dried shrimp, soaked in
    warm water for 10 minutes
15ml/1 tbsp coarsely chopped garlic
1 hard-boiled egg, chopped
4 shallots, thinly sliced into rings
fresh coriander (cilantro) leaves and
    2 fresh red chillies, seeded and sliced,
    to garnish

FOR THE DRESSING
30ml/2 tbsp fresh lime juice
5ml/1 tsp palm sugar (jaggery) or
    light muscovado (brown) sugar
30ml/2 tbsp Thai fish sauce

1 Preheat the oven to 180°C/350°F/ Gas 4. Prick the aubergines with a skewer, then arrange on a baking sheet. Place directly on the shelf of the oven for about 1 hour, turning at least twice, until charred and tender. Remove and set aside until cool enough to handle. Then peel off the skin and cut the flesh into slices.

2 Meanwhile, make the dressing. Put the lime juice, sugar and fish sauce into a bowl. Whisk well with a fork. Cover with clear film (plastic wrap) and set aside until required.

3 Heat the oil in a small frying pan. Drain the shrimp and add to the pan with the garlic. Cook over a medium heat for 3 minutes, until golden. Remove from the pan and set aside.

4 Carefully arrange the roasted aubergine slices on a serving dish. Top with the hard-boiled egg, shallots and dried shrimp mixture.

5 Drizzle the dressing over the salad. Garnish with coriander and sliced chillies.

Nutritional information per portion: Energy 90Kcal/376kJ; Protein 7.2g; Carbohydrate 4.7g, of which sugars 4.3g; Fat 4.9g, of which saturates 0.9g; Cholesterol 86mg; Calcium 113mg; Fibre 3g; Sodium 612mg.

Thai prawn salad with garlic dressing and frizzled shallots

In this intensely flavoured salad, juicy prawns and sweet mango are partnered with a sweet-and-sour garlic dressing which is heightened with the hot taste of chilli. The crispy frizzled shallots are a traditional addition to Thai salads.

SERVES 4–6

675g/1¹/₂lb medium raw prawns (shrimp), peeled
    and deveined, with tails intact
finely shredded rind of 1 lime
¹/₂ fresh red chilli, seeded and
    finely chopped
30ml/2 tbsp olive oil, plus extra
    for brushing
1 ripe but firm mango
2 carrots, cut into long thin shreds
10cm/4in piece cucumber, sliced
1 small red onion, halved and thinly sliced
45ml/3 tbsp roasted peanuts, coarsely chopped

4 large shallots, thinly sliced and fried until crisp
    in 30ml/2 tbsp groundnut (peanut) oil
salt and ground black pepper

FOR THE DRESSING
1 large garlic clove, chopped
10–15ml/2–3 tsp caster
    (superfine) sugar
juice of 2 limes
15–30ml/1–2 tbsp Thai fish sauce
1 fresh red chilli, seeded and
    finely chopped
5–10ml/1–2 tsp light rice vinegar

1 Place the prawns in a non-metallic dish with the lime rind, chilli, oil and seasoning. Toss to mix thoroughly and leave to marinate at room temperature for 30–40 minutes.

2 Make the dressing. Place the garlic in a mortar with 10ml/2 tsp of the caster sugar. Pound with a pestle until smooth, then work in about three-quarters of the lime juice, followed by 15ml/1 tbsp of the Thai fish sauce.

3 Transfer the dressing to a jug (pitcher). Stir in half the chopped red chilli. Taste the dressing and add more sugar, lime juice and/or fish sauce, if you think they are necessary, and stir in light rice vinegar to taste.

4 Peel and stone (pit) the mango. The best way to do this is to cut either side of the large central stone (pit), as close to it as possible, with a sharp knife. Cut the flesh into very fine strips and cut off any flesh still adhering to the stone.

5 Place the mango in a bowl and add the carrots, cucumber and red onion. Pour over about half the dressing and toss thoroughly. Arrange the salad on four to six individual plates or bowls.

6 Heat a ridged, cast-iron griddle pan or heavy frying pan until very hot. Brush with a little oil, then sear the marinated prawns for 2–3 minutes on each side, until they turn pink and are patched with brown on the outside. Arrange the prawns on the salads.

7 Sprinkle the remaining dressing over the salads. Sprinkle over the remaining chilli with the peanuts and crisp-fried shallots. Serve immediately.

Nutritional information per portion: Energy 292Kcal/1222kJ; Protein 33.5g; Carbohydrate 13.4g, of which sugars 11.8g; Fat 11.9g, of which saturates 2g; Cholesterol 329mg; Calcium 160mg; Fibre 2.7g; Sodium 596mg.

Scented fish salad

For a tropical taste of the Far East, try this delicious fish salad scented with coconut, fruit and warm Thai spices. Do try to locate the pitaya or dragon fruit. The flesh of this fruit is sweet and refreshing, with a slightly acidic melon-like flavour that goes particularly well with fish.

SERVES 4

350g/12oz fillet of red mullet,
    sea bream or snapper
1 cos or romaine lettuce
1 papaya or mango, peeled and sliced
1 pitaya, peeled and sliced
1 large ripe tomato, cut into wedges
1/2 cucumber, peeled and cut into batons
3 spring onions (scallions), sliced
salt

FOR THE MARINADE
5ml/1 tsp coriander seeds
5ml/1 tsp fennel seeds

2.5ml/1/2 tsp cumin seeds
5ml/1 tsp caster (superfine) sugar
2.5ml/1/2 tsp hot chilli sauce
30ml/2 tbsp garlic oil

FOR THE DRESSING
60ml/4 tbsp coconut milk
60ml/4 tbsp groundnut (peanut) oil
finely grated rind and juice of 1 lime
1 red chilli, seeded and finely chopped
5ml/1 tsp granulated (white) sugar
45ml/3 tbsp chopped fresh coriander (cilantro)

1 Cut the fish into even strips, removing any stray bones. Place it on a plate.

2 Make the marinade. Put the coriander, fennel and cumin seeds in a mortar. Add the sugar and crush with a pestle. Stir in the chilli sauce, garlic oil, and salt to taste and mix to a paste. Spread the paste over the fish, cover and leave to marinate in a cool place for at least 20 minutes.

3 Make the dressing. Place the coconut milk and salt in a screw-top jar. Add the oil, lime rind and juice, chilli, sugar and coriander. Shake well.

4 Wash and dry the lettuce leaves. Place in a bowl and add the papaya or mango, pitaya, tomato, cucumber and spring onions. Pour in the dressing and toss well to coat.

5 Heat a large non-stick frying pan, add the fish and cook for 5 minutes, turning once. Add the cooked fish to the salad, toss lightly and serve immediately.

Nutritional information per portion: Energy 304Kcal/1269kJ; Protein 17.6g; Carbohydrate 11.7g, of which sugars 11.6g; Fat 21.1g, of which saturates 3.6g; Cholesterol 0mg; Calcium 89mg; Fibre 2.6g; Sodium 88mg.

Rice salad

The sky's the limit with this recipe. Use whatever fruit, vegetables and even leftover meat that you might have, mix with cooked rice and serve with the fragrant dressing.

SERVES 4–6

350g/12oz/3 cups cooked rice
1 Asian pear, cored and diced
50g/2oz dried shrimp, chopped
1 avocado, peeled, stoned (pitted)
   and diced
1/2 cucumber, finely diced
2 lemon grass stalks, finely chopped
30ml/2 tbsp sweet chilli sauce
1 fresh green or red chilli, seeded and
   finely sliced
115g/4oz/1 cup flaked (sliced)
   almonds, toasted
small bunch fresh coriander
   (cilantro), chopped
fresh Thai sweet basil leaves, to garnish

FOR THE DRESSING
300ml/1/2 pint/11/4 cups water
10ml/2 tsp shrimp paste
15ml/1 tbsp palm sugar (jaggery)
   or light muscovado (brown) sugar
2 kaffir lime leaves, torn into small pieces
1/2 lemon grass stalk, sliced

1 Make the dressing. Put the measured water in a small pan with the shrimp paste, sugar, kaffir lime leaves and lemon grass.

2 Heat gently, stirring continuously, until the sugar dissolves, then bring to boiling point and simmer for 5 minutes.

3 Strain the mixture into a bowl and set aside until cold.

4 Put the cooked rice into a salad bowl and fluff up the grains with a fork.

5 Add the Asian pear, dried shrimp, avocado, cucumber, lemon grass and sweet chilli sauce. Mix well.

6 Add the sliced chilli, almonds and coriander to the bowl and toss well. Garnish with Thai basil leaves and serve with the bowl of dressing.

Nutritional information per portion: Energy 404Kcal/1689kJ; Protein 16.1g; Carbohydrate 36.7g, of which sugars 8.5g; Fat 22.4g, of which saturates 2.6g; Cholesterol 63mg; Calcium 247mg; Fibre 4g; Sodium 550mg.

Tangy chicken salad

This fresh and lively dish typifies the character of Thai cuisine. It is ideal for a light lunch on a hot and lazy summer's day. The creamy coconut dressing is the perfect contrast to the spicy chilli.

SERVES 4–6

4 skinless, boneless chicken breasts
2 garlic cloves, crushed
30ml/2 tbsp soy sauce
30ml/2 tbsp vegetable oil
120ml/4fl oz/¹/₂ cup coconut cream
30ml/2 tbsp Thai fish sauce
juice of 1 lime
30ml/2 tbsp palm sugar (jaggery) or
   light muscovado (brown) sugar
115g/4oz/¹/₂ cup water chestnuts, sliced
50g/2oz/¹/₂ cup cashew nuts, roasted
   and coarsely chopped
4 shallots, thinly sliced
4 kaffir lime leaves, thinly sliced
1 lemon grass stalk, thinly sliced
5ml/1 tsp chopped fresh galangal
1 large fresh red chilli, seeded and
   finely chopped
2 spring onions (scallions), thinly sliced
10–12 fresh mint leaves, torn
1 lettuce, roughly sliced
2 fresh red chillies, seeded
   and sliced, to garnish

1 Place the chicken in a large dish. Rub with the garlic, soy sauce and 15ml/1 tbsp of the oil. Cover and leave to marinate for 1–2 hours.

2 Heat the remaining oil in a wok or frying pan. Stir-fry the chicken for 3–4 minutes on each side, or until cooked. Set aside to cool.

3 In a pan, heat the coconut cream, fish sauce, lime juice and sugar. Stir until the sugar dissolves; set aside.

4 Tear the cooked chicken breasts into strips and put them in a bowl. Add the water chestnuts, cashew nuts, shallots, kaffir lime leaves, lemon grass, galangal, chopped red chilli, spring onions and mint leaves to the chicken.

5 Pour the coconut dressing over the mixture and toss well. Arrange the lettuce on serving plates, place the salad on top and garnish with the sliced red chillies.

Nutritional information per portion: Energy 404Kcal/1691kJ; Protein 40.4g; Carbohydrate 11.3g, of which sugars 9g; Fat 22.3g, of which saturates 9.8g; Cholesterol 105mg; Calcium 25mg; Fibre 0.8g; Sodium 666mg.

Saeng wa of grilled pork

Pork fillet is cut in strips before being grilled. Shredded and then tossed with a delicious sweet-sour sauce, it makes a marvellous warm salad.

SERVES 4

30ml/2 tbsp dark soy sauce

15ml/1 tbsp clear honey

400g/14oz pork fillet (tenderloin)

6 shallots, very thinly sliced lengthways

1 lemon grass stalk, thinly sliced

5 kaffir lime leaves, thinly sliced

5cm/2in piece fresh root ginger, peeled
    and sliced into fine shreds

1/2 fresh long red chilli, seeded and sliced
    into fine shreds

small bunch fresh coriander
    (cilantro), chopped

FOR THE DRESSING

30ml/2 tbsp palm sugar (jaggery) or
    light muscovado (brown) sugar

30ml/2 tbsp Thai fish sauce

juice of 2 limes

20ml/4 tsp thick tamarind juice, made by
    mixing tamarind paste with warm water

1 Preheat the grill (broiler) to medium. Mix the soy sauce with the honey in a small bowl or jug (pitcher) and stir until the honey has completely dissolved.

2 Cut the pork fillet lengthways into quarters to make four long, thick strips. Place in a grill pan. Brush generously with the soy sauce and honey mixture, then grill (broil) for 10–15 minutes, until cooked through and tender. Turn the strips over frequently and baste with the soy sauce and honey mixture.

3 Transfer the cooked pork strips to a chopping board. Slice the meat across the grain, then shred it with a fork. Place in a large bowl and add the shallot slices, lemon grass, kaffir lime leaves, ginger, chilli and chopped coriander.

4 Make the dressing. Place the sugar, fish sauce, lime juice and tamarind juice in a bowl. Whisk together until the sugar has completely dissolved. Pour the dressing over the pork mixture and toss well to mix, then serve.

Nutritional information per portion: Energy 170Kcal/718kJ; Protein 22g; Carbohydrate 12.2g, of which sugars 12.1g; Fat 4g, of which saturates 1.4g; Cholesterol 63mg; Calcium 16mg; Fibre 0.2g; Sodium 873mg.

Beef and mushroom salad

All of the ingredients you will need to make this traditional Thai dish – known as yam nua yang *– are widely available in larger supermarkets.*

SERVES 4

675g/1½lb fillet (tenderloin) or
    rump (round) steak
30ml/2 tbsp olive oil
2 small mild red chillies, seeded
    and sliced
225g/8oz/3¼ cups shiitake mushrooms,
    stems removed and caps sliced

FOR THE DRESSING

3 spring onions (scallions),
    finely chopped
2 garlic cloves, finely chopped
juice of 1 lime
15–30ml/1–2 tbsp Thai fish sauce
5ml/1 tsp soft light brown sugar
30ml/2 tbsp chopped fresh
    coriander (cilantro)

TO SERVE

1 cos or romaine lettuce, torn
    into strips
175g/6oz cherry tomatoes, halved
5cm/2in piece cucumber, peeled,
    halved and thinly sliced
45ml/3 tbsp toasted
    sesame seeds

1 Preheat the grill (broiler) to medium, then cook the steak for 2–4 minutes on each side. (In Thailand, beef is traditionally served quite rare.) Leave the steak to cool for at least 15 minutes.

2 Slice the meat as thinly as possible and place the slices in a bowl.

3 Heat the olive oil in a small frying pan. Add the seeded and sliced red chillies and the sliced shiitake mushroom caps. Cook for 5 minutes, stirring occasionally.

4 Turn off the heat and add the steak slices to the pan. Stir well to coat the steak slices in the chilli and mushroom mixture.

5 Make the dressing by mixing all the ingredients together in a bowl, then pour it over the meat mixture and toss gently.

6 Arrange the lettuce, tomatoes and cucumber on a serving plate. Spoon the steak mixture on to the centre of the salad and sprinkle the sesame seeds over the top. Serve at once.

Nutritional information per portion: Energy 381Kcal/1588kJ; Protein 39.7g; Carbohydrate 4g, of which sugars 3.8g; Fat 23g, of which saturates 6.6g; Cholesterol 103mg; Calcium 105mg; Fibre 2.4g; Sodium 352mg.

Larp of Chiang Mai

Chiang Mai is a city in the north-east of Thailand. The city is culturally very close to Laos and is famous for its chicken salad.

SERVES 4–6

450g/1lb minced (ground) chicken
1 lemon grass stalk, root trimmed
3 kaffir lime leaves, finely chopped
4 fresh red chillies, seeded and chopped
60ml/4 tbsp fresh lime juice
30ml/2 tbsp Thai fish sauce
15ml/1 tbsp roasted ground rice
2 spring onions (scallions),
    finely chopped
30ml/2 tbsp fresh coriander (cilantro) leaves
thinly sliced kaffir lime leaves, mixed salad leaves
    and fresh mint sprigs, to garnish

1 Heat a large, non-stick frying pan. Add the minced chicken and moisten with a little water. Stir constantly over a medium heat for 7–10 minutes, until it is cooked through. Remove the pan from the heat and drain off any excess fat. Cut off the lower 5cm/2in of the lemon grass stalk and chop it finely.

2 Transfer the cooked chicken to a bowl and add the chopped lemon grass, lime leaves, chillies, lime juice, fish sauce, roasted ground rice, spring onions and coriander. Mix thoroughly.

3 Spoon the chicken mixture into a salad bowl. Sprinkle sliced lime leaves over the top and garnish with salad leaves and sprigs of mint.

Nutritional information per portion: Energy 135Kcal/572kJ; Protein 27.4g; Carbohydrate 3.4g, of which sugars 0.4g; Fat 1.3g, of which saturates 0.4g; Cholesterol 79mg; Calcium 8mg; Fibre 0.1g; Sodium 424mg.

Thai beef salad

A hearty main course salad, this combines tender strips of sirloin steak with a wonderfully piquant chilli and lime dressing.

SERVES 4

2 sirloin steaks, each about 225g/8oz
1 lemon grass stalk, root trimmed
1 red onion or 4 Thai shallots, thinly sliced
1/2 cucumber, cut into strips
30ml/2 tbsp chopped spring onion (scallion)
juice of 2 limes
15–30ml/1–2 tbsp Thai fish sauce
2–4 fresh red chillies, seeded and finely chopped
Chinese mustard cress, salad cress or fresh coriander
    (cilantro), to garnish

1 Fry the steaks in a large frying pan over a medium heat. Cook for 4–6 minutes for rare, 6–8 minutes for medium-rare and 10 minutes for well done, depending on their thickness. Alternatively, cook under a preheated grill (broiler). Remove the steaks from the pan and leave to rest for 10–15 minutes. Meanwhile, cut off the lower 5cm/2in from the lemon grass stalk and chop finely.

2 When the meat is cool, slice thinly and put in a large bowl. Add the sliced onion or shallots, cucumber, lemon grass and chopped spring onion to the meat slices.

3 Toss the salad and add lime juice and fish sauce to taste. Add the red chillies and toss again. Transfer to a serving bowl or plate. Serve the salad at room temperature or chilled, garnished with the Chinese mustard cress, salad cress or coriander leaves.

Nutritional information per portion: Energy 161Kcal/674kJ; Protein 26.9g; Carbohydrate 1.8g, of which sugars 1.4g; Fat 5.1g, of which saturates 2.3g; Cholesterol 57mg; Calcium 14mg; Fibre 0.3g; Sodium 347mg.

Desserts

After a Thai meal, it is customary to serve

fresh fruits, sometimes carved into

beautiful shapes, to cleanse the palate.

Ices are popular too, especially when

based on watermelon or coconut.

However, Thais also love sticky

sweetmeats, and these are often prettily

presented on palm leaves or decorated

with tiny flowers.

Coconut and lemon grass ice cream

Here the combination of cream and coconut milk makes for a wonderfully rich ice cream. The lemon grass flavouring is very subtle, but quite delicious.

SERVES 4

2 lemon grass stalks
475ml/16fl oz/2 cups double
   (heavy) cream
120ml/4fl oz/½ cup coconut milk

4 large (US extra large) eggs
105ml/7 tbsp caster
   (superfine) sugar
5ml/1 tsp vanilla extract

1 Cut the lemon grass stalks in half lengthways. Use a mallet or rolling pin to mash the pieces, breaking up the fibres so that all the flavour is released.

2 Pour the cream and coconut milk into a pan. Add the lemon grass stalks and heat gently, stirring frequently, until the mixture starts to simmer.

3 Put the eggs, sugar and vanilla extract in a large bowl. Using an electric whisk, whisk until the mixture is very light and fluffy.

4 Strain the cream mixture into a heatproof bowl that will fit over a pan of simmering water. Whisk in the egg mixture, then place the bowl over the pan and continue to whisk until the mixture thickens. Remove it from the heat and leave to cool. Chill the coconut custard in the refrigerator for 3–4 hours.

5 Pour the mixture into a plastic tub or similar freezerproof container. Freeze for 4 hours, beating two or three times at hourly intervals with a fork to break up the ice crystals.

6 Alternatively, use an ice cream maker. Pour the chilled mixture into the machine and churn until firm. Serve immediately, or scrape into a freezerproof container and store in the freezer.

7 About 30 minutes before serving, transfer the container to the refrigerator so that the ice cream softens slightly. Serve in scoops.

Nutritional information per portion: Energy 787Kcal/3261kJ; Protein 9.6g; Carbohydrate 30.9g, of which sugars 30.9g; Fat 70.5g, of which saturates 41.6g; Cholesterol 391mg; Calcium 115mg; Fibre 0g; Sodium 145mg.

Watermelon ice

After a hot and spicy Thai meal, the only thing more refreshing than ice-cold watermelon is this watermelon ice. The kaffir lime leaves enhance the subtle fragrance of the fruit.

SERVES 4–6

**90ml/6 tbsp caster
   (superfine) sugar**
105ml/7 tbsp water
**4 kaffir lime leaves, torn into
   small pieces**
500g/1¼lb watermelon

1 Put the sugar, water and lime leaves in a pan. Heat gently until the sugar has dissolved. Pour into a large bowl and set aside to cool.

2 Cut the watermelon into wedges. Cut the flesh from the rind, remove the seeds and chop. Spoon the watermelon into a food processor. Process to a slush, mix with the sugar syrup and chill in the refrigerator for 3–4 hours.

3 Strain into a freezerproof container. Freeze for 2 hours, then beat with a fork to break up the ice crystals. Freeze for 3 hours more, beating at half-hourly intervals. Freeze until firm. Alternatively, use an ice cream maker. Pour the chilled mixture into the machine and churn until firm enough to scoop.

4 Serve immediately, or scrape into a freezerproof container and store in the freezer. About 30 minutes before serving, transfer the ice to the refrigerator so that it softens slightly and is easier to scoop.

Nutritional information per portion: Energy128Kcal/545kJ; Protein 0.8g; Carbohydrate 32.4g, of which sugars 32.4g; Fat 0.4g, of which saturates 0.1g; Cholesterol 0mg; Calcium 21mg; Fibre 0.1g; Sodium 4mg.

Coconut custard

This traditional dessert can be baked or steamed and is often served with sweet sticky rice and a selection of fresh fruit. Mangoes and tamarillos go particularly well with the custard and rice.

SERVES 4

4 eggs
75g/3oz/6 tbsp soft light brown sugar
250ml/8fl oz/1 cup coconut milk
5ml/1 tsp vanilla, rose or
    jasmine extract
icing (confectioners') sugar, to decorate
sliced fruit, to serve

1 Preheat the oven to 150°C/300°F/Gas 2. Whisk the eggs and sugar in a bowl until smooth. Add the coconut milk and extract and whisk well.

2 Strain the mixture into a jug (pitcher), then pour it into four individual heatproof glasses, ramekins or an ovenproof dish.

3 Stand the glasses, ramekins or dish in a roasting pan. Fill the pan with hot water to reach halfway up the sides of the ramekins or dish.

4 Bake for about 35–40 minutes, or until the custards are set. Test with a fine skewer or cocktail stick (toothpick). Remove the roasting pan from the oven, lift out the ramekins or dish and leave to cool.

5 If you like, turn out the custards on to serving plate(s). Decorate with a dusting of icing sugar, and serve with sliced fruit.

Nutritional information per portion: Energy 161Kcal/681kJ; Protein 6.5g; Carbohydrate 22.7g, of which sugars 22.7g; Fat 5.7g, of which saturates 1.7g; Cholesterol 190mg; Calcium 57mg; Fibre 0g; Sodium 140mg.

Mango and lime fool

Canned mangoes are used here for convenience, but the dish tastes even better if made with fresh ones. Choose a variety like the voluptuous Alphonso mango, which is wonderfully fragrant.

SERVES 4

400g/14oz can sliced mango
grated rind of 1 lime
juice of ¹/₂ lime
150ml/¹/₄ pint/²/₃ cup double
    (heavy) cream

90ml/6 tbsp Greek (US strained
    plain) yogurt
fresh mango slices,
    to decorate (optional)

1 Drain the canned mango slices and put them in the bowl of a food processor. Add the grated lime rind and the lime juice. Process until the mixture forms a smooth purée. Alternatively, mash the mango slices with a potato masher, then press through a sieve (strainer) into a bowl with the back of a wooden spoon. Stir in the lime rind and juice.

2 Pour the cream into a bowl and add the yogurt. Whisk until the mixture is thick and then quickly whisk in the mango mixture.

3 Spoon into four tall cups or glasses and chill for 1–2 hours. Just before serving, decorate each glass with fresh mango slices, if you like.

Nutritional information per portion: Energy 269Kcal/1118kJ; Protein 2.8g; Carbohydrate 15.2g, of which sugars 14.9g; Fat 22.6g, of which saturates 13.8g; Cholesterol 51mg; Calcium 64mg; Fibre 2.6g; Sodium 26mg.

Papayas in jasmine flower syrup

The fragrant syrup can be prepared in advance, using fresh jasmine flowers from a house plant or the garden. It tastes fabulous with papayas, but it is also good with all sorts of desserts.

SERVES 2

105ml/7 tbsp water
45ml/3 tbsp palm sugar (jaggery) or
   light muscovado (brown) sugar
20–30 jasmine flowers, plus a
   few extra, to decorate (optional)
2 ripe papayas
juice of 1 lime

1 Place the water and sugar in a small pan. Heat gently, stirring occasionally, until the sugar has dissolved, then simmer, without stirring, over a low heat for 4 minutes.

2 Pour into a bowl, leave to cool slightly, then add the jasmine flowers. Leave to steep for at least 20 minutes.

3 Peel the papayas and slice in half lengthways. Scoop out and discard the seeds. Place the papayas on serving plates and sprinkle over the lime juice.

4 Strain the jasmine syrup into a clean bowl, discarding the flowers. Spoon the syrup over the papayas. If you like, decorate with a few fresh jasmine flowers.

Nutritional information per portion: Energy 215Kcal/914kJ; Protein 1.9g; Carbohydrate 54.3g, of which sugars 54.3g; Fat 0.4g, of which saturates 0g; Cholesterol 0mg; Calcium 93mg; Fibre 7.7g; Sodium 19mg.

Coconut cream diamonds

Desserts like these are widely popular across South-east Asia. Commercially ground rice can be used but grinding jasmine rice yourself – in a food processor – gives a much better result.

SERVES 4–6

75g/3oz/scant 1/2 cup jasmine rice,
   soaked overnight in 175ml/6fl oz/
   3/4 cup water
350ml/12fl oz/1 1/2 cups coconut milk
150ml/1/4 pint/2/3 cup single
   (light) cream
50g/2oz/1/4 cup caster
   (superfine) sugar
raspberries and fresh mint leaves,
   to decorate

FOR THE COULIS

75g/3oz/3/4 cup blackcurrants,
   stalks removed
30ml/2 tbsp caster
   (superfine) sugar
75g/3oz/1/2 cup fresh or
   frozen raspberries

1 Put the rice and its soaking water into a food processor and process for a few minutes until soupy.

2 Heat the coconut milk and cream in a non-stick pan. When at boiling point, stir in the rice. Cook over a very gentle heat for 10 minutes, stirring constantly. Stir in the sugar and cook for a further 10–15 minutes, or until thick and creamy.

3 Line a rectangular tin (pan) with non-stick baking parchment. Pour the coconut rice mixture into the pan, cool, then chill in the refrigerator until set and firm.

4 Meanwhile, make the coulis. Put the blackcurrants in a bowl and sprinkle them with the sugar. Set aside for 30 minutes. Turn the fruit into a sieve (strainer) set over a bowl. Using a spoon, press the fruit against the sieve so that the juices collect in the bowl. Taste and add more sugar if necessary.

5 Cut the coconut cream into diamonds. Spoon a little of the coulis on to each dessert plate, arrange the coconut cream diamonds on top and decorate with the raspberries and mint. Serve immediately.

Nutritional information per portion: Energy 252Kcal/1067kJ; Protein 3.4g; Carbohydrate 44.2g, of which sugars 28.1g; Fat 8.2g, of which saturates 4.9g; Cholesterol 21mg; Calcium 95mg; Fibre 1.2g; Sodium 110mg.

Stewed pumpkin in coconut milk

Fruit stewed in coconut milk is a popular dessert in Thailand. Pumpkins, bananas and melons can all be prepared in this way.

SERVES 4–6

1kg/2¼lb kabocha pumpkin
750ml/1¼ pints/3 cups
    coconut milk
175g/6oz/¾ cup granulated (white) sugar
pinch of salt
4–6 fresh mint sprigs, to decorate

1 Cut the pumpkin in half using a large, sharp knife, then cut away and discard the skin. Scoop out the seed cluster. Reserve a few seeds and throw away the rest. Using a sharp knife, cut the pumpkin flesh into pieces that are about 5cm/2in long and 2cm/¾in thick.

2 Wash the reserved pumpkin seeds, pat dry and toast them in a dry frying pan, or spread on a baking sheet and grill (broil) until golden brown, tossing frequently.

3 Pour the coconut milk into a pan. Add the sugar and salt and bring to the boil. Add the pumpkin and simmer for about 10–15 minutes, until it is tender. Serve warm, in individual dishes. Decorate each serving with a mint sprig and toasted pumpkin seeds.

Nutritional information per portion: Energy 246Kcal/1051kJ; Protein 2.5g; Carbohydrate 60.4g, of which sugars 59.2g; Fat 1.1g, of which saturates 0.6g; Cholesterol 0mg; Calcium 150mg; Fibre 2.5g; Sodium 209mg.

Mangoes with sticky rice

Sticky or glutinous rice is just as good in desserts as in savoury dishes, and mangoes complement it especially well.

SERVES 4

115g/4oz/²⁄₃ cup white glutinous rice
175ml/6fl oz/¾ cup thick coconut milk
45ml/3 tbsp granulated (white) sugar
pinch of salt
2 ripe mangoes
strips of pared lime rind, to decorate

1 Rinse the rice in several changes of cold water, then leave to soak overnight in a bowl of fresh cold water. Drain the rice well and spread out in a steamer lined with muslin (cheesecloth). Cover and steam over a pan of simmering water for 20 minutes, or until tender.

2 Reserve 45ml/3 tbsp of the cream from the top of the coconut milk. Pour the remainder into a pan and add the sugar and salt. Heat, stirring constantly, until the sugar has dissolved, then bring to the boil. Remove from the heat, pour into a bowl and leave to cool.

3 Turn the rice into a bowl and pour over the cooled coconut milk. Stir well, then leave to stand for 10–15 minutes. Meanwhile, peel the mangoes, cut the flesh away from the central stones (pits) and cut into slices.

4 Spoon the rice on to plates. Arrange the mango slices on one side, then drizzle with the coconut cream. Decorate with strips of lime rind and serve.

Nutritional information per portion: Energy 200Kcal/846kJ; Protein 3.1g; Carbohydrate 46g, of which sugars 24.3g; Fat 0.8g, of which saturates 0.2g; Cholesterol 0mg; Calcium 32mg; Fibre 2g; Sodium 51mg.

Coconut pancakes

These light and sweet pancakes are often served as street food by the hawkers in Bangkok. They are quick and easy and make a delightful dessert.

MAKES 8

75g/3oz/¾ cup plain (all-purpose) flour, sifted

60ml/4 tbsp rice flour

45ml/3 tbsp caster (superfine) sugar

50g/2oz/⅔ cup desiccated (dry unsweetened shredded) coconut

1 egg

275ml/9fl oz/generous 1 cup coconut milk

vegetable oil, for frying

lime wedges and maple syrup, to serve

1 Place the flours, sugar and coconut in a bowl, stir to mix and then make a well in the centre. Break the egg into the well and pour in the coconut milk.

2 With a whisk or fork, beat the egg into the coconut milk and then gradually whisk in the surrounding dry ingredients until the mixture forms a batter. The mixture will not be entirely smooth but there shouldn't be any large lumps.

3 Heat a little oil in a small non-stick frying pan. Pour in about 45ml/3 tbsp of the mixture and spread to a thin layer with the back of a spoon. Cook over a high heat for 30–60 seconds, until bubbles appear on the surface of the pancake, then turn over and cook the other side until golden.

4 Slide each pancake on to a plate and keep warm. Serve warm with lime wedges and maple syrup.

Nutritional information per portion: Energy 183Kcal/763kJ; Protein 2.9g; Carbohydrate 23.1g, of which sugars 6.9g; Fat 9g, of which saturates 4.1g; Cholesterol 24mg; Calcium 33mg; Fibre 1.4g; Sodium 49mg.

Steamed custard in nectarines

Steaming nectarines or peaches brings out their natural colour and sweetness, so this is a good way of making the most of underripe or less flavourful fruit.

SERVES 4–6

6 nectarines
1 large (US extra large) egg
45ml/3 tbsp palm sugar (jaggery) or
   light muscovado (brown) sugar
30ml/2 tbsp coconut milk

1 Cut the nectarines in half. Using a teaspoon, carefully scoop out the stones (pits) and a little of the surrounding flesh.

2 Lightly beat the egg, then add the sugar and the coconut milk. Beat until the sugar has dissolved.

3 Place the nectarines in a steamer and carefully fill the cavities three-quarters full with the custard mixture. Steam over a pan of simmering water for 5–10 minutes until set. Remove from the heat and leave to cool before transferring to plates and serving.

Nutritional information per portion: Energy 150Kcal/637kJ; Protein 5g; Carbohydrate 29.7g, of which sugars 29.7g; Fat 2.2g, of which saturates 0.6g; Cholesterol 67mg; Calcium 32mg; Fibre 2.4g; Sodium 36mg.

Fried bananas

These deliciously sweet treats are a favourite with children and adults alike. In Thailand, you will find them on sale from roadside stalls and markets at almost every hour of the day and night.

SERVES 4

115g/4oz/1 cup plain
   (all-purpose) flour
2.5ml/¹/₂ tsp bicarbonate of soda
   (baking soda)
pinch of salt
30ml/2 tbsp granulated (white) sugar
1 egg, beaten
90ml/6 tbsp water
30ml/2 tbsp desiccated (dry unsweetened
   shredded) coconut or 15ml/1 tbsp
   sesame seeds
4 firm bananas
vegetable oil, for deep-frying
30ml/2 tbsp clear honey,
   to serve (optional)

1 Sift the flour, bicarbonate of soda and salt into a large bowl. Stir in the sugar and the egg, and whisk in enough of the water to make a thin batter. Whisk in the coconut or sesame seeds so that they are evenly distributed.

2 Peel the bananas. Carefully cut each one in half lengthways, then in half crossways to make 16 pieces of about the same size. Don't do this until you are ready to cook them because, once peeled, bananas quickly discolour.

3 Heat the oil in a large pan, wok or deep-fryer to 190°C/375°F or until a cube of bread, dropped in the oil, browns in about 45 seconds. Dip the banana pieces in the batter, then gently drop a few into the oil. Deep-fry until golden brown, then lift out and drain on kitchen paper.

4 Cook the remaining banana pieces in the same way. Serve immediately with honey, if using.

Nutritional information per portion: Energy 462Kcal/1930kJ; Protein 6.2g; Carbohydrate 53.4g, of which sugars 29.2g; Fat 26.2g, of which saturates 3.4g; Cholesterol 48mg; Calcium 83mg; Fibre 2.3g; Sodium 21mg.

Thai fried pineapple

This is a very simple and quick Thai dessert. The slightly sharp taste of the fruit makes it a very refreshing treat at the end of a meal, especially when served with creamy yogurt.

SERVES 4

1 pineapple
40g/1½oz/3 tbsp butter
15ml/1 tbsp shredded coconut
60ml/4 tbsp soft light brown sugar
60ml/4 tbsp fresh lime juice
lime slices, to decorate
thick and creamy natural (plain) yogurt,
   to serve

1 Using a sharp knife, cut the top off the pineapple and peel off the skin, taking care to remove the eyes. Cut it in half and remove and discard the woody core. Cut the flesh lengthways into 1cm/½in wedges.

2 Heat the butter in a large, heavy frying pan or wok. When it has melted, add the pineapple wedges and cook over a medium heat for 1–2 minutes on each side, or until they have turned pale golden in colour.

3 Meanwhile, dry-fry the coconut in a small frying pan until lightly browned. Remove from the heat and set aside.

4 Sprinkle the sugar into the pan with the pineapple, add the lime juice and cook, stirring constantly, until the sugar has dissolved. Divide the pineapple wedges among four bowls, sprinkle with the coconut, decorate with the lime slices and serve with the yogurt.

Nutritional information per portion: Energy 228Kcal/960kJ; Protein 1.1g; Carbohydrate 33.7g, of which sugars 33.7g; Fat 10.9g, of which saturates 7.2g; Cholesterol 21mg; Calcium 42mg; Fibre 2.6g; Sodium 66mg.

Tapioca pudding

This pudding, made from large pearl tapioca and coconut milk and served warm, is much lighter than the Western-style version. You can adjust the sweetness to your taste. Serve with lychees or the smaller, similar-tasting longans – also known as "dragon's eyes".

SERVES 4

115g/4oz/²/₃ cup tapioca
475ml/16fl oz/2 cups water
175g/6oz/³/₄ cup granulated
   (white) sugar
pinch of salt

250ml/8fl oz/1 cup coconut milk
250g/9oz prepared tropical fruits
finely shredded lime rind and
   shaved fresh coconut (optional),
   to decorate

1 Put the tapioca in a bowl and pour over warm water to cover. Leave to soak for 1 hour so the grains swell. Drain.

2 Pour the measured water into a large pan and bring to the boil over a medium heat. Add the sugar and salt and stir until dissolved.

3 Add the tapioca and coconut milk, return to the boil, then reduce the heat to low and simmer gently for 10 minutes, or until the tapioca becomes transparent.

4 Spoon into one large or four individual bowls and serve warm with the tropical fruits. Decorate with the lime rind and coconut shavings, if using.

Nutritional information per portion: Energy 325Kcal/1388kJ; Protein 1g; Carbohydrate 84.9g, of which sugars 57.4g; Fat 0.4g, of which saturates 0.2g; Cholesterol 0mg; Calcium 51mg; Fibre 1.8g; Sodium 74mg.

Baked rice pudding, Thai-style

Black glutinous rice, also known as black sticky rice, has long dark grains and a nutty taste reminiscent of wild rice. This baked pudding has a distinct character and flavour all of its own, as well as an intriguing appearance.

SERVES 4–6

175g/6oz/1 cup black or white
   glutinous rice
30ml/2 tbsp soft light brown sugar
475ml/16fl oz/2 cups coconut milk

250ml/8fl oz/1 cup water
3 eggs
30ml/2 tbsp granulated (white) sugar

1 Combine the glutinous rice and brown sugar in a pan. Pour in half the coconut milk and the water.

2 Bring to the boil, reduce the heat to low and simmer, stirring occasionally, for 15–20 minutes, or until the rice has absorbed most of the liquid. Preheat the oven to 150°C/300°F/Gas 2.

3 Spoon the rice mixture into a single large ovenproof dish or divide it among individual ramekins. Beat the eggs with the remaining coconut milk and sugar in a bowl.

4 Strain the egg mixture into a jug (pitcher), then pour it evenly over the par-cooked rice in the dish or ramekins.

5 Place the dish or ramekins in a roasting pan. Carefully pour in enough hot water to come halfway up the sides of the dish or ramekins.

6 Cover with foil and bake for about 35–60 minutes, or until the custard has set. Serve warm or cold.

Nutritional information per portion: Energy 292Kcal/1226kJ; Protein 8.8g; Carbohydrate 52.7g, of which sugars 19.9g; Fat 5.2g, of which saturates 1.4g; Cholesterol 143mg; Calcium 70mg; Fibre 0g; Sodium 185mg.

The Thai kitchen

Fresh fish from the sea, rice from the

fields, aromatic herbs and spices and

locally grown fruits and vegetables are

just a few of the wonderful ingredients

that are enjoyed throughout Thailand.

While each region has its own

specialities, there are common

flavourings and culinary techniques

that are used all over the country.

Thai cuisine

Founded on simple ingredients of excellent quality, food is regarded by Thai people as an important daily pleasure. Thai cuisine relies on five primary flavours that are used in differing proportions to produce a wonderful range of dishes. The cooking of each region, while using these basic flavours, has its own characteristics and produces an interesting array of local specialities.

The influence of the Royal Palace, which placed an equal importance on the flavour and appearance of food, is still seen in the preparation of Thai dishes today, particularly in their carefully crafted presentation and decoration.

ABOVE: *A Thai cook prepares a classic stir-fried dish in her kitchen.*

NORTHERN CUISINE

Unlike the rest of Thailand, where jasmine rice is favoured, northerners prefer sticky glutinous rice, which can be rolled into balls and dipped into sauces or curries. The curries are often thin because coconut milk, which is used as a thickener elsewhere, is not readily available. The dishes also tend to be less spicy than in other regions. Unusual ingredients found in the north include buffalo meat and giant beetles.

The influence of Burma and Laos can be found in many northern dishes. The chicken curry, koi soi, and the popular pork curry, gaeng hong lae, originated in Burma. Nam prik nuum, a smoky, not-too-spicy dip served with poached freshwater fish and crisp fried pork, shows a Laotian influence.

The traditional entertainment in northern Thailand is the *kantoke* dinner (*kan* means bowl). Guests sit on the floor around a low table and serve themselves various dishes, which are constantly replaced by the host.

FOOD IN THE NORTH-EAST

North-eastern Thais have a reputation for adventurous eating. Some of the more unusual delicacies include ant

THE FIVE FLAVOURS

In Thai cooking, the five key flavours that are used are salty, sweet, sour, bitter and hot.

Salty

This enhances and brings out the tastes of the other ingredients. It is not usually added in the form of table salt, but through salty ingredients. One of the most widely used of these is nam pla, a sauce made from fermented fish, while kapi, a salty shrimp paste, is used to add its own flavour to dishes.

Sweet

Thai food often has a subtle sweetness. Sweet ingredients such as palm sugar (jaggery) are often added to savoury dishes to enhance the flavours of spices and herbs. Honey is sometimes also used as a sweetener.

Sour

Lime juice is one of the most popular sour flavourings because it also helps to accentuate other flavours. Sour tamarind, often sold as wet tamarind, is also used as a souring agent. Various vinegars are also employed.

Bitter

The bitter flavour of Thai dishes is produced by ingredients such as herbs or dark green vegetables.

Hot

Despite the fiery reputation of Thai cuisine, not all dishes are hot. The main source of heat is the chilli, which is sold fresh, dried or in pastes and sauces (priks). Heat can also be introduced through ginger, onions and garlic. Chilli-based condiments are placed on the table so that diners can add further heat to their own taste.

eggs, grubworms, grasshoppers, snail curry and pungent, fermented fish. While many people in Thailand look down on the eating habits of the north-easterners, restaurants in Bangkok prepare many north-eastern specialities such as som tam (green papaya salad), laap, a dish of spiced raw minced (ground) meat, and haw mok pla, a fish custard steamed in banana leaves.

EATING IN THE CENTRAL REGION

The traditional food of this region, particularly in the outlying villages, is often plainer than that eaten elsewhere. A typical dish will consist of rice with stir-fried vegetables, fish from a nearby river, canal or paddy field, and a salad made from salted eggs, chillies, spring onion (scallion) and lime juice.

In Bangkok you can experience not only Thailand's regional cuisines, but also many international dishes.

SOUTHERN COOKING

Fish and shellfish are abundant in the south, which is almost completely surrounded by coastline. Many traditional dishes feature rock lobsters, crabs, mussels, squid, prawns (shrimp) and scallops. They may be used in soup, grilled (broiled), steamed, or added to a curry.

Many different cultures and countries have influenced this region of Thailand, and there is a strong Muslim presence, which can be seen in the food. Mussaman-style curry shows a definite Indian influence, while satay originates from Indonesia.

Coconuts grow plentifully everywhere, providing milk for thickening soups and curries, and oil for frying. Cashew nuts and pineapples also grow here. In general, the food is chilli-hot.

BELOW: *A Thai woman enjoys a bowl of rice at a bustling floating market. Markets are a feature of Thai life.*

THE ROYAL PALACE TRADITION

The tradition of food decoration and presentation originates from the court of the Grand Palace in Bangkok. Living within the walls of the inner palace was a large community of women who existed almost independently from the outside world. Aristocrats and noblemen vied for their daughters to be taken into the palace, where they would receive training in the running of an elegant household, honing and refining skills that would impress potential husbands.

An integral part of their training was learning to prepare food. Importance was laid equally between flavour and aesthetic appeal. Many hours were spent on painstaking preparation, perfecting the flavour and appearance of each dish.

One of the most visually impressive skills passed down through generations of these women was that of vegetable and fruit carving. The women learned to transform various vegetables and fruits into the most intricate creations. Huge watermelons and tiny chillies were turned into elaborate blossoming flowers, and pumpkins and ginger roots were cut into complicated abstract designs or pretty birds.

As times and attitudes changed, the Grand Palace gradually evolved and the polygamous environment was finally abolished under the reign of King Rama VI, but the skills of cooks still survive today.

Rice

The most important ingredient in Thai cooking is rice. In fact when people are called to the table, the phrase used – gkin kao – literally translates as "a time to eat rice". All the other foods that make up a meal – meat, fish and vegetables – are regarded as accompaniments and are referred to as ghap kao or "things eaten with rice".

The average Thai eats 158kg/350lb of rice every year, which is almost a pound a day. It is consumed in various forms, from basic steamed rice to rice noodles, crackers and cakes.

Two distinct types of rice are popular in Thailand. The first is a delicately scented long grain variety, which is used as a staple and is eaten at all meals. It comes in several qualities, and is white and fluffy with separate grains when cooked. In northern Thailand, a starchy glutinous rice is preferred. When cooked, the grains stick together.

Rice mother

The traditional rice-growing communities in Thailand have a high regard for *Mae Pra Posop*, the "Rice Mother". Elaborate ceremonies are performed in her name during various stages of rice cultivation so that she may bless the fields with bountiful harvests from year to year.

ABOVE: *Glutinous rice, which may be black (although, more accurately, it is a very dark red), white or a hybrid known as "jasmine sweet", is most widely used in north and north-eastern Thailand.*

The best quality rice is harvested in December, when the cool, dry weather allows the grains to ripen slowly. At other times of the year, the vagaries of the climate can cause problems. If the weather is too hot, the grains may ripen prematurely; if it is too wet, there is a chance that the rice may develop mould on the husks.

JASMINE RICE (Khao chao)

Also known as fragrant or scented rice, this long grain variety is the staple food of the central and southern parts of Thailand. As the name suggests, it has a delicate aroma. The flavour is slightly nutty, and it resembles Basmati rice from India. The uncooked grains are translucent and, when cooked, the rice is fluffy and white. Most of the crop comes from a region between central and north-

RIGHT: *Jasmine or Thai fragrant rice has tender, aromatic grains and is the preferred rice throughout the central and southern parts of the country. It is widely available in supermarkets and Asian stores in the West.*

eastern Thailand where the soil is a combination of clay and sand. Newly harvested rice from this region, which is sometimes eaten as a delicacy, is prized for the tender and delicate texture of the grains.

GLUTINOUS RICE (Kao niow)

Commonly referred to as sweet or sticky rice, this is the mainstay of the diet in the northern and north-eastern regions of the country. It is delicious and very filling. Its name is derived entirely from its sticky texture, as rice does not contain any gluten. Easily cultivated on the hillsides and high plateaux of these regions, glutinous rice requires less water during the growing period than the rice of the central lowlands (sometimes known as "wet rice").

Glutinous rice comes in both short or round grain and long grain varieties. Thai people prefer the long grain variety; the short grain rice is usually used in Japanese and Chinese cooking. Some of the long grain varieties have a delicate, aromatic flavour, and these high-grade hybrids are sometimes labelled "jasmine

sweet" or "jasmine glutinous rice", which indicates they have something in common with the fragrant, non-glutinous jasmine rice.

What makes this type of rice unusual is the way in which the grains clump together when they are cooked. This enables the rice to be eaten with the hands. The starchiness of glutinous rice gives the uncooked grain a distinct opaque white colour, which is different from the more translucent appearance of regular rice grains. When soaked and steamed, however, the reverse is true. Glutinous rice becomes translucent, while regular rice turns opaque. Although it is in the north and the north-eastern regions of Thailand that glutinous rice is most popular, it is also eaten elsewhere in the country, most frequently in sweet snacks or desserts.

BLACK GLUTINOUS RICE (Kao niow dam)

This wholegrain rice – that is, with only the husk removed – has a rich, nutty flavour that is distinctly different from the more subtle taste of white glutinous rice. It is generally sweetened with coconut milk and sugar and eaten as a snack or dessert, rather than being used as the staple of a savoury meal. It does tend to be quite heavy, filling and indigestible if eaten in quantity, so it is usually nibbled as a sweetmeat snack in the mid-afternoon or later in the evening, after the evening meal has been digested. A popular version of roasted glutinous rice, flattened into a cake, is khao mow rang, which is sold at markets throughout Thailand.

In spite of its name, black rice isn't actually black in colour. If the grains are soaked in water for a few hours, the water will turn a deep burgundy red, showing the rice's true colour.

RICE PRODUCTS
Fermented rice (Khao mak)

Made by fermenting cooked glutinous rice, this is a popular sweetmeat, sold by street vendors.

Rice-pot crust (Khao tang)

In several cultures, the crust that forms on the base of the pan when rice is cooked in a particular way is highly prized. In Thailand, the crust is lifted off the base of the pan in sheets and dried out in the sun before being sold. Khao tang is toasted or fried before being eaten.

To make khao tang, spread a layer of cooked rice 5mm/³⁄₄in thick on a greased baking sheet. Dry it out in a low oven, 140°C/275°F/Gas 1, for several hours. Cool, then break into pieces. Deep-fry until puffed, but not browned, then drain on kitchen paper.

ABOVE: *On deep-frying, rice squares puff up into crispy crackers.*

Dry rice squares

These can be purchased at Asian food stores. When fried in hot oil, they puff up into crispy rice crackers in the same way as prawn (shrimp) crackers.

Rice flour (paeng khao jao and paeng khao niao)

This flour may be made from either glutinous or non-glutinous raw rice that has been very finely ground. It is used to make the dough for fresh rice noodles and is also used to make desserts such as pancakes. Rice flour is readily available in Asian food stores. When the source is non-glutinous rice it is called paeng khao jao and when the flour is made from glutinous rice it is known as paeng khao niao. Store it in an airtight container as you would ordinary wheat flour.

ABOVE: *Rice flour is finely ground and pulverized. As a result, it has a light texture and is used in desserts such as pancakes.*

PREPARING AND COOKING RICE

Rice is a staple of Thai cooking and it should be cooked to perfection. Jasmine (or Thai fragrant) rice is best cooked using the absorption or covered pan method, which maximizes its fragrant flavour. Glutinous rice, in contrast, requires a slightly different cooking method involving long soaking followed by steaming.

Rinsing

Jasmine rice should always be rinsed thoroughly before being cooked as this helps to remove excess starch and any dust that may have accumulated during storage.

1 Put the jasmine rice in a large bowl and pour in sufficient cold water to cover. Gently swirl the grains between your fingers. As you do so, the water will become slightly cloudy.

2 Leave the rice to settle, then tilt the bowl so that the water drains away. Alternatively, strain the rice and return it to the bowl. Cover the rice once more with cold water, then swirl the grains again, leave to settle and drain. Repeat the rinsing several times – at least three – until the water runs clear. Drain well before cooking.

Cooking by the absorption method

Also known as the covered pan method, jasmine rice is cooked in a measured amount of water until all the water has been absorbed. The proportion of rice to water, and the cooking time, will depend on the type of rice used, but as a guide, you will need about 600ml/1 pint/2½ cups for every 225g/8oz/generous 1 cup rice.

1 Put the rice into a pan and pour in the measured water. Do not add salt. Bring to the boil, then reduce the heat to the lowest possible setting.

2 Cover tightly with a lid and cook until the liquid has been absorbed, up to about 25 minutes.

3 Remove the pan from the heat. Leave the lid on the pan and leave it to stand in a warm place for about 5 minutes or until tender.

Adding flavourings

If you want to add a little flavour to the rice, the absorption method of cooking it provides the perfect opportunity. Simply add herbs or spices, such as lemon grass or fresh root ginger, with the liquid.

To add even more flavour to the rice, substitute either coconut milk or stock for the water – or use a mixture.

Cooking rice to perfection

• When cooking rice, it is essential that the pan is covered tightly. If the lid of your pan is loose, cover the pan with foil or a clean dish towel before fitting the lid, making sure that any excess fabric is kept well away from the heat source.

• The rice must be cooked on a very low heat – don't be tempted to increase the heat during cooking to speed the process or the water may evaporate before the rice is fully cooked.

• Leave rice to stand for 5 minutes after cooking and before serving to "rest" it and complete the cooking process. If it isn't completely tender, re-cover the pan and leave for 5 minutes more.

• Remember that rice absorbs water as it cooks. If you use too much water with the absorption method, or cook the rice for too long, it will become soggy.

• If cooked rice is required for a fried rice dish, cook it by the absorption method, cool quickly, then chill it before frying.

Cooking by the microwave method

Although no faster than conventional cooking, using the microwave is a convenient way of preparing Thai rice.

1 Using the same proportions as for the absorption method, put the rice in a microwave-safe container. Add the boiling measured liquid, without any salt.

2 Cover and cook on full power for 10–15 minutes, or according to the manufacturer's instructions. Leave to stand, without stirring, for 10 minutes.

Cooking using an electric rice cooker

Put the rice into the cooker and add the required amount of water as indicated in your instruction booklet. Do not add salt. Cover the cooker and switch it on. The cooker will switch itself off automatically when the rice is ready, and will keep the rice warm.

Cooking by steaming

This is a combination of two cooking methods: the rice is partially cooked in a pan of simmering water, then drained and steamed. This method is used for plain jasmine rice. It is also suitable for some glutinous rice dishes.

1 Cook the rice by the absorption method for three-quarters of the normal cooking time. Drain the partially cooked rice.

2 Put the rice in a sieve (strainer) or steamer, lined with muslin (cheesecloth), set over a pan of simmering water. Cover tightly and steam for 10 minutes. If the grains still feel slightly hard in the centre, steam for a little longer.

Making jasmine rice pudding

This is a quick dessert for four. Cook 50g/2oz/1/4 cup jasmine rice in 475ml/16fl oz/2 cups boiling water until the water has been absorbed and the rice is tender. Leave for a few minutes, then stir in 120ml/4fl oz/1/2 cup milk and a little caster (superfine) sugar to taste. Serve hot.

STORING RICE

Packets of rice can be kept in a cool, dark place for up to three years if unopened. Alternatively, store the rice in an airtight container. Cooked rice can be stored for up to 24 hours if cooled quickly, covered and kept in the refrigerator. The cooled rice can also be frozen for up to 3 months.

COOKING GLUTINOUS RICE

Glutinous rice should be soaked before cooking for 1–4 hours. The rice is then best cooked by steaming it for 10–15 minutes, until tender.

Making glutinous rice pudding

Glutinous rice can be simmered with coconut milk and sugar to make a delicious dessert for four.

1 In a bowl, cover 75g/3oz/scant 1/2 cup glutinous rice with cold water and leave to soak for 3–4 hours. Drain and put in a pan with 300ml/1/2 pint/11/4 cups milk or coconut milk.

2 Bring to the boil, then lower the heat, cover and simmer for 25–30 minutes. Add sugar, coconut cream and any flavourings to taste, and cook uncovered for 5–10 minutes more until the rice is tender.

Food safety

Never keep cooked rice warm for more than a short time, or you may risk food poisoning. Rice is susceptible to a bacterium *Bacillus cereus*, which is killed by cooking, but can leave behind spores that germinate if cooked rice is kept warm for long periods.

Noodles

Second only to rice in importance in the Thai diet, noodles are consumed in large quantities, are cooked in a number of ways and are eaten at any time of day, including breakfast.

There are basically five main varieties of noodles used in Thai cooking: sen ya, ba mee, sen mee, sen lek and wun sen. They come either fresh or dried and in several sizes, from tiny transparent threads to large sheets. Many of them are made from rice but other types of noodles are based on wheat flour or flour made from ground mung beans.

RICE NOODLES (Kui teow)

Both fresh and dried rice noodles are available in Thai markets. Fresh ones are highly perishable and must be cooked as soon as possible after purchase. Rice noodles are available in a wide range of shapes and widths.

Noodle know-how

Both dried and fresh noodles have to be cooked in boiling water before use – or soaked in boiling water until pliable. How long for depends on the type of noodle, the thickness and whether or not the noodles are going to be cooked again. As a rule, after soaking, dried noodles require 3 minutes' cooking, while fresh ones will need a minute and may require rinsing to prevent overcooking.

Vermicelli rice noodles (Mee)

These noodles are usually sold dried and must be soaked in boiling water before use. When dried, rice vermicelli is called sen mee or rice stick noodles.

Medium rice noodles (Kui teow sen lek)

Resembling spaghetti, these noodles are usually sold dried. The city of Chanthaburi is famous for sen lek noodles, which are sometimes called Jantoboon noodles after the nickname for the town.

Rice stick noodles (Kui teow sen yai)

Also known as rice river noodles, these are sold both dried and fresh, although the latter form is more popular. When fresh they tend to be rather sticky and need to be separated before being cooked.

Rice noodle nests (Khanom chine)

Despite the allusion to China in the name, these fresh thick round noodles are a Thai speciality, made of rice flour.

Khanom chine are white and the strands are a little thicker than spaghetti. At most markets in Thailand, nests of these noodles are a familiar sight. They are sold freshly cooked. You buy them by the hundred nests and should allow four or five

ABOVE: *Rice stick noodles are flat, not unlike Italian tagliatelle.*

nests per person. Fresh noodles are highly perishable: buy them early in the day, and steam them again at home. They can be served with nam ya, nam prik and a variety of curries.

Preparing rice noodles

Rice noodles need only to be soaked in hot water for a few minutes to soften them before serving. Add the noodles to a large bowl of just-boiled water and leave for 5–10 minutes, or until they soften, stirring occasionally to separate the strands. If the noodles are soaked for too long, they will become soggy. Their dry weight will usually double after soaking, so 115g/4oz dry noodles will produce about 225g/8oz after soaking.

LEFT: *Dried vermicelli rice noodles should be soaked, not boiled.*

Making deep-fried rice noodles

Rice stick noodles puff up and become wonderfully crisp when they are deep-fried. To prepare, place the noodles in a large bowl and soak in cold water for 15 minutes. Drain the noodles and lay them on kitchen paper to dry.

Heat about 1.2 litres/2 pints/5 cups vegetable oil in a large, high-sided frying pan or wok to 180°C/350°F. To test if the oil is ready, carefully drop in a couple of noodle strands. If they puff and curl up immediately, the oil is hot enough. Carefully add a handful of dry noodles to the oil. When they puff up, after about 2 seconds, flip them over with a long-handled strainer and cook for 2 seconds more. Transfer to a baking sheet lined with kitchen paper to cool. Fry just a handful of noodles at a time. The noodles will stay crisp for about 2 days if stored in a sealed plastic bag. Allow to go cold before storing.

BELOW: *Egg noodles are available dried and fresh in the West.*

EGG NOODLES (Ba mee)

These noodles owe their yellow colour to the egg used in their manufacture. Sold fresh in nests, they must be shaken loose before being cooked. Very thin ones are known as egg thread noodles. The flat noodles are used for soups and the rounded type are for stir-frying.

Cooking egg noodles

Cook egg noodles in boiling water for 4–5 minutes, or according to the packet instructions. Drain and serve.

CELLOPHANE NOODLES (Wun sen)

These thin, wiry noodles, also called glass, jelly or bean thread noodles, are made from mung beans. They are the same size as mee but are transparent. They are only available dried.

Preparing cellophane noodles

Cellophane noodles are never served on their own, but always as an ingredient in a dish. Soak them in hot water for 10–15 minutes to soften them, then drain and cut into shorter strands.

WRAPPERS

These are used throughout Thailand to wrap around a filling. Some may be eaten fresh while others are deep-fried.

Wonton wrappers (Baang giow)

Originally Chinese, these thin yellow pastry squares are made from egg and wheat flour and can be bought fresh or frozen. Fresh wrappers will last for about five days, double-wrapped and stored in the refrigerator. Simply peel off the number you require. Frozen wrappers should be thawed before use.

Rice paper (Banh trang)

These brittle, semi-transparent, paper-thin sheets are made from a mixture of rice flour, water and salt, rolled out by a machine until very thin and then dried in the sun. Packets of 50–100 sheets are available. Store in a cool, dry place. Before use, dip in water until pliable, then wrap around a filling to make fresh spring rolls, or deep-fry.

Spring roll wrappers (Bang hor)

These wafer-thin wrappers are used to make classic Chinese spring rolls. The wrapper sizes available range from 8cm/3¼in to 30cm/12in square, and they usually come in packets of 20. Once opened, they will dry out quickly, so peel off one at a time and keep the rest covered.

BELOW: *Spring roll wrappers are made from a wheat and water dough.*

Vegetables

Bursting with flavour and nutrients, Thai cooks use vegetables freely in stir-fries and braised dishes. There is always a wide variety of vegetables to choose from in Thai markets.

AUBERGINES/EGGPLANTS (Makhua ling)

Aubergines may be oval, tubular or round. Asian aubergines tend to be smaller than European ones, ranging from the size of a pea to the size of a tennis ball. Colours range from white to green, orange, purple and black. Four varieties are used today.

ABOVE: *Thai aubergines are usually small and fairly round in shape.*

Long aubergines (Makhua yaew)

This elongated variety is served grilled (broiled) or in green curries.

Apple aubergines (Makhua khun)

These small round varieties are pale green, yellow or white. They are eaten raw with chilli sauce, nam prik, or cooked in curries. They are eaten for their texture rather than flavour.

Pea aubergines (Makreu puang)

These pea-size berries have a bitter flavour that is a good foil to the richness of spicy curries. They are also used as a flavouring for nam prik.

Hairy aubergines (Maeuk)

These aubergines are orange in colour and have to have the hairs scraped off before being pounded to flavour nam prik. They have a sour taste. Any sour fruit can be used as a substitute.

Preparing aubergines

Wash the aubergine and remove the stalk, then cut into slices, strips or chunks. Some recipes recommend salting aubergine for 30 minutes before cooking. This is not necessary if the vegetables are young and tender.

BAMBOO SHOOTS (Nor mai pai tong)

The creamy white shoots of some species of the bamboo plant are sold diced, chopped, shredded or whole in cans. Before using the canned shoots, drain and rinse them well.

ABOVE: *Tiny pea aubergines are bright green and grow in clusters.*

BEANS
Long beans (Thua fak yao)

Also called yard-long beans or snake beans, long beans resemble green beans but are longer. The two common varieties are pale green and dark green.

Winged beans (Tua phuu)

Usually only the young pods are eaten. They are blanched and served with coconut milk, cooked in oil and eaten with nam prik, or sliced finely and used as an ingredient in tod man, keing phed and spicy salads. Use regular green beans or asparagus as a substitute.

ABOVE: *Bamboo shoots are available fresh or sliced and canned.*

Twisted cluster beans (Parkia or sa-taw)

The seeds of a huge tree that grows in southern Thailand, these beans are about the size of broad (fava) beans. The bright green pods that house them are flat and wavy. The beans are eaten as a vegetable, and they taste good in a sweet-and-sour stir-fry. They are also roasted and eaten with nam prik, and are made into pickles.

ABOVE: *Mung and soya beansprouts are widely used in Thai cooking.*

BEANSPROUTS (Thua ngok)

Many types of bean can be sprouted, but the sprouts most often used in Thai cooking are the small "green" sprouts from mung beans and the larger "yellow" sprouts from soya beans. Fresh beansprouts are widely available in supermarkets, health stores and Asian food stores, or you can sprout your own beans at home.

Preparing beansprouts

To prepare fresh beansprouts, rinse them in cold water to remove the husks and tiny roots. They can be eaten raw, blanched or briefly stir-fried. Do not overcook them.

MUNG BEANS

These tiny beans are usually green, although some varieties are yellow or black. They are available from supermarkets and health stores. They are a good source of protein and vitamins and are used in both savoury dishes and desserts.

BABY CORN COBS (Khaao phot on)

Corn is a popular vegetable in Thailand and roasted cobs are often on sale from street vendors. For stir-fries and soups, Thais prefer baby corn cobs, which have a musty sweet flavour, as well as a crunchy texture. They are available fresh and canned.

Preparing corn cobs

If using canned corn cobs, rinse them under cold water and drain them well. They can usually be used whole but if they are quite large, cut them in half lengthways or slice them diagonally into chunks.

Take care not to overcook them as they will lose their crisp texture. Blanch fresh corn cobs for 1 minute in lightly salted, boiling water and drain before stir-frying.

ABOVE: *Baby corn cobs are tender and sweet – the first choice for stir-fries.*

PAK CHOI/BOK CHOY (Hua ka-lum pee)

This is the most popular variety of cabbage eaten in Thailand. It is often eaten raw with a chilli dipping sauce and is also cooked in stir-fries and soups. Pak choi is thinly sliced and is best cooked briefly.

LEFT: *Pak choi has a wonderfully crisp texture and delightful peppery flavour.*

CHINESE LEAVES/CHINESE CABBAGE (Phak kaet khaao-plee)

Also known as celery cabbage, this vegetable has soft green and white leaves with a mild, sweet flavour and a crisp texture.

FLOWERING CABBAGE (Phak kwaang tung)

This type of cabbage has a delicate flavour and is usually cut into short lengths and used in soups and noodle dishes, but it may also be stir-fried.

CHINESE CELERY (Kean ghai)

This is similar to Western celery, but the stems are thinner and their flavour is more pronounced. The leaves are often used in soups.

ABOVE: *Angled loofah has a sweet, delicate flavour when young.*

ANGLED LOOFAHS (Buap liam)

Also known as silk gourd, silk squash or Chinese okra, this dark green vegetable looks like a courgette (zucchini) or a large okra pod, and has angular ridges down its length. A close relative, the smooth loofah is paler in colour, larger and more cylindrical, with a thicker base. Both have a mild taste, similar to cucumber, which can be used in its place in most cooked dishes. Loofah is used in stir-fries and soups, and is often boiled and eaten with nam prik. It is always eaten cooked, but be careful not to overcook it.

BITTER MELON (Mara)

Also known as Chinese bitter gourd, this resembles a knobbly cucumber, with about 10 ridges running along its length. Before it ripens, the melon is pale green in colour, and it is at this stage that its flesh is particularly prized. The Thais believe that it is very good for the kidneys and blood. It can be added to soups or curries. Alternatively, blanch in salted, boiling water for 2 minutes before use.

WAX GOURDS/FUZZY MELON (Taeng)

These gourds come in several shapes, from a short stubby variety to one that looks like a long, fuzzy cucumber. In fact, an alternative name is hairy cucumber. The most common variety is cylindrical in shape. They can be boiled and eaten with nam prik, or added to a soup flavoured with pork bones. They are fairly bland in flavour.

MOOLI/DAIKON (Hua phak kaak)

Thais value this vegetable, believing that it aids digestion, cools the body and improves blood circulation. Also called giant white radish or winter radish, it is a long white root that resembles a slender, smooth-skinned parsnip in appearance. When raw, the flavour of mooli is cool, sharp and peppery, and the texture is crisp. Thais don't often eat it this way, but the grated flesh is sometimes used to tenderize seafood. When the vegetable is cooked, the characteristic texture is retained, but the flavour of mooli becomes quite sweet.

ABOVE: *Water chestnuts can be bought fresh as dark brown corms, or canned.*

ABOVE: *Mooli is usually cooked in Thailand, rather than served raw as in Japan.*

LOTUS ROOTS (Rak bua)

Fresh lotus roots grow in sausage-like links, each one about 18–23cm/7–9in long. (Strictly speaking, they are rhizomes rather than roots.) Once the mud that coats them has been washed off, a pale beige-pink skin is revealed. Lotus root is available canned and frozen, although neither is quite as crunchy as the fresh root. For salads and stir-fries, lotus root must first be blanched in boiling water, although it can be added directly to soups or stews. As it cooks, it will sweeten the liquid and turn it a pale pink. Thin slices of lotus root can also be deep-fried to make crisps (US chips). Dry the rounds thoroughly before adding them to the hot oil.

WATER CHESTNUTS (Haew)

Nothing beats the crisp texture and nutty, sweet flavour of a fresh water chestnut. The corm of a grass-like plant, water chestnuts are encased in dark brown skin which must be peeled before the familiar white vegetable is revealed. In Thai cooking, water chestnuts are used in salads, stir-fries and even in desserts.

YAM BEANS (Mun kaew)

In the Americas, where it originated, this popular vegetable is known as jicama. The vegetable looks like a large brown turnip. The flesh is sweet and crunchy and the flavour is a cross between apple and potato. Yam bean is best eaten raw with a spicy dip, although it is used in stir-fries and in desserts. It may be eaten as a fruit.

TARO (Puak)

This root grows wild on the banks of streams in Thailand and is particularly popular in the north of the country. The swollen tuber is full of starch and is eaten in the same manner as potatoes. The young leaves can also be eaten. Wear gloves when you are peeling taros.

RIGHT: *Taro is a rough-skinned tuber that grows wild.*

ONIONS (Hua hom)

Onions are not as popular as shallots in Thai cooking and those that are on sale tend to be fairly small. Yellow in colour, they are quite pungent, with a sweet, peppery flavour. Many Thai dishes are garnished with crisp-fried onion flakes. You can buy these ready-fried onions in tubs from some Thai or other Asian grocery stores.

Spring onions/scallions (Ton horm)

Spring onions are used in Thai cooking for stir-fries and in soups. They are

ABOVE: *Shallots from Thailand are small, pinky purple in colour, quite pungent and not as juicy as onions.*

also popular for garnishes, either sliced or cut into tassels, then curled in iced water.

Shallots (Horn dang)

Thai shallots are smaller and much more pungent than those used in the West. Pinkish purple in colour, they are used extensively in Thai cooking to flavour relishes, soups, stews and curries, and are also sliced into rings and deep-fried as a garnish. Shallots are sweeter, much milder and not as juicy as onions, and they are often used with other aromatic ingredients, such as fresh chillies, garlic and dried shrimp, to make the spice pastes for which Thailand is so famous.

CHINESE CHIVES (Kui chai)

These pungent herbs look more like long, flat spring onions than their Western equivalent. The leaves are peppery, crunchy and chewy. Chinese chives are eaten both raw and cooked and are highly prized for both their texture and flavour.

Making crispy shallots

It is very important to deep-fry the shallots slowly or they will not cook evenly.

1 Peel 10–15 Thai shallots, slice them thinly and separate the slices into rings.

2 Heat 475ml/16fl oz/2 cups of oil in a deep frying pan over a medium heat until hot. Add the shallots and cook for 15–20 minutes until golden brown.

3 Cool slightly, then strain the oil into a bowl. Spread the shallots out on a baking sheet lined with kitchen paper and leave to cool completely.

MORNING GLORY (Pakk boog)

This popular leafy plant, also known as water spinach, is actually a herb. It grows in marshy areas, near rivers and canals, and is related to the morning glory that riots over walls and fences in many European gardens. The flavour is similar to that of spinach.

ABOVE: *Morning glory, which has a flavour that is reminiscent of spinach, is widely eaten throughout Thailand.*

Mushrooms

There are many different varieties of both fresh and dried mushrooms – hed – used in Thai cooking. As well as cultivated mushrooms, wild mushrooms are gathered during the rainy season, especially in the north of Thailand. These include ceps, chanterelles and russulas, which are used for salads, soups and sauces.

STRAW MUSHROOMS (Hed fang)

These delicate, sweet-flavoured mushrooms have acquired their English name because of the method of cultivation on beds of straw. They look like miniature helmets and are the most popular variety of mushroom in Thai cooking. Straw mushrooms are used extensively in soups, salads and

BELOW: Canned straw mushrooms, though not as tasty, can be used as a substitute for fresh ones as these are not often readily available in the West.

curries, and taste particularly good with prawns (shrimp) and crab meat. Canned straw mushrooms are widely available from Asian stores and many supermarkets. They have neither the exquisite flavour nor the texture of the fresh mushrooms, but can be an acceptable substitute. Fresh straw mushrooms are highly perishable and so are not often available in the West. If you do locate them, use them as soon as possible after purchase.

LEFT: Shiitake mushrooms are available both dried, as preferred by Thai cooks, and fresh.

SHIITAKE MUSHROOMS (Hed hom)

Fresh shiitake mushrooms are available, but Thai cooks prefer to use them dried as they have a stronger flavour and more texture. Both types are found in supermarkets and Asian stores. Dried shiitake mushrooms must be reconstituted in water before being used. The stems are usually discarded and the caps sliced or chopped for adding to soups or stews. The soaking water can be strained and used in a soup or stock as it takes on the flavour of the shiitake. The dried mushrooms will keep well if they are stored in a sealed plastic tub or bag in a cool, dry place.

ABOVE: Dried wood ear mushrooms are valued for their texture. They readily absorb the flavours of other ingredients.

DRIED WOOD EAR, TREE EAR OR CLOUD EAR (Hed hunu heang)

Although often described as dried mushrooms, these should really be called fungi. They look like dried leaves. When soaked in boiling water, they revive, puff up and stretch into shiny black, rubbery caps. When soaked, the fungus expands to six or eight times its volume, so be sure to use plenty of water. After soaking, leave the mushrooms to cool, then pinch off and discard the hard stems. Drain, rinse, then drain again, and discard any hard roots and grit. The mushrooms can be cooked whole or thinly sliced for soups and stir-fries.

Reconstituting dried mushrooms

To reconstitute dried mushrooms, soak them in boiling water for 20–30 minutes, depending on the variety and size, until tender. Drain and rinse well to remove any grit and dirt. They can now be stir-fried, braised, steamed or used in soups. Dried mushrooms often need to be cooked for a little longer than fresh ones.

Tofu

This excellent and inexpensive protein food was invented by the Chinese and is now widely enjoyed throughout the world as a healthy alternative to fish and meat. Tofu is low in sugar and fat.

Tofu – tow hoo – is a product of the yellow soya bean. The beans are soaked, husked and pounded with water to produce soya milk. The milk is then filtered, boiled and curdled, using gypsum, to produce the solid cakes of beancurd we know as tofu.

ABOVE: *(clockwise from top) Pressed, silken and firm tofu.*

ABOVE: *Pressed tofu has a firm texture and is used in pad Thai (fried noodles).*

Two types of fresh tofu are now widely available. Silken tofu is very soft and is often used in soups. The firmer white cakes of tofu can stand up to more rigorous handling, although even these need to be handled with care. Both types come packaged in water, either in tubs or vacuum packed. Ideally, tofu should be used straightaway, but, if it is kept submerged in water, which is changed daily, it can be stored in the refrigerator for 3–4 days.

There are numerous other tofu products that are also very popular in Thai cooking.

PRESSED TOFU (Taohu kao)

This is a fresh beancurd cake that has had almost all the moisture squeezed out of it, leaving a solid block with a smooth texture. Brown outside and white inside, it is often seasoned with soy sauce and may also be smoked.

DRIED BEANCURD SKIN (Fong taohu hang)

This can be purchased at Asian food stores. It consists of thin sheets of curd that are skimmed off simmering soya milk and dried. They are sold either flat or rolled to form beancurd sticks. The skins can also be used in casseroles, soups or stir-fries, while the sticks are popular in vegetarian dishes.

Dried beancurd skins need to be soaked in cold water before they can be used. The sheets require soaking for 1–2 hours, but the sticks should be soaked for at least several hours, preferably overnight.

ABOVE: *Originally from Indonesia, tempeh is now popular in Thai cooking.*

DEEP-FRIED TOFU (Tau hoo tord)

When tofu is deep-fried in hot oil, it puffs up and turns golden brown, the flavour intensifies and the texture becomes chewy. Cubes of deep-fried tofu are sold in Asian markets. Store in the refrigerator and use within 3 days. The cubes absorb other flavours well, and they make a good meat substitute, especially in a stir-fry.

PICKLED TOFU OR BEAN PASTE (Tow hoo yee)

This product is made by fermenting fresh tofu, then drying it in the sun before marinating it in an alcohol mixture. The curd can be red or white and the flavour is extremely powerful. The best pickled beancurd comes from China and is sold in bottles or jars.

TEMPEH

This solid beancurd is an Indonesian speciality made by fermenting cooked soya beans with a cultured starter. It resembles firm tofu, but has a slightly nutty, more savoury taste. It benefits from a marinade.

Fruit

Tropical fruits grow widely in Thailand. Eat them on their own or, in typical Thai style, serve them as a palate-cleansing dessert.

BANANAS (Kluai)

Indigenous to Thailand, the banana plant is actually a huge herb. The stem makes a delicious curry and the buds, when cooked, taste like artichokes.

Over 30 different varieties of banana grow in Thailand, from small rice bananas to the large, bright yellow Cavendish Gros Michael. Flavour varies too, from mild to sweet and fragrant.

Cooking bananas, or plantains, have firm pinkish flesh. They must be cooked before being eaten. In Thailand they are used in curries.

Banana buds (Hua plee)

Also called banana flowers and banana blossoms, these are the tender hearts of unopened banana flowers, which have been stripped of their purple petals. They are available fresh in some Asian markets and canned or dried.

ABOVE: *At the heart of the banana flower lies the delicate banana bud.*

PAPAYAS (Malako)

There are two main varieties in Thailand: khak nuan, a blunt cylindrical papaya with a yellow skin and sweet orange flesh, and wuak dam, also cylindrical but with a pointed end. Its skin and sweet flesh is reddish.

Ripe papaya is often served simply sprinkled with lime juice. The unripe fruit is usually treated as a vegetable, and may be boiled or enjoyed raw in salads or as a relish.

MANGOES (Ma muang)

There are several varieties of mango; some are grown as dessert fruit, others for eating or cooking while still green. Ok-rong is a dessert fruit with a pale yellow skin, a small variety that fits easily in the palm of the hand. Although somewhat stringy, the very sweet and fragrant flavour makes

ok-rong an excellent companion for coconut sticky rice. Another popular variety is the nam dawg mai (meaning "nectar of flowers"), a delightfully fragrant, juicy mango. The skin is smooth and thin, enclosing delicate, string-free flesh around a thin seed. The mango most often eaten green is ma-muang mun. This has a nutty taste, unlike the sour young green mangoes used in sauces and salads.

ABOVE: *Papayas can be cooked or eaten raw and are widely used in both sweet and savoury dishes throughout Thailand.*

Banana leaves

These large pliable green leaves are used extensively in Thai cooking to wrap food for steaming, roasting and grilling (broiling). During the cooking process the leaves impart a mild smoky flavour to the food. Sometimes they will tinge it a very light green as well. The leaves are also used for presentation, as mats, for lining dishes, as platters and to make attractive containers that can be secured with bamboo picks.

RIGHT: *When very ripe, small apple bananas have a faint taste and aroma of fresh apple.*

ABOVE: *Guavas are scented with a sweet-sharp flavour.*

GUAVAS (Farang)

Many varieties of this fruit are found in Thailand. The most popular is the lemon guava. This round, greenish-yellow fruit weighs about 225g/8oz and has a hard white flesh with small whitish-brown seeds that are generally discarded before eating. The Thais eat the fruit before it becomes over-ripe and develops its characteristic acidic, scented flavour. At this stage, the flesh is crisp and tastes rather bland, but is good dipped in a chilli sauce. For a simple dessert, sprinkle slices of guava with sugar, cover closely and leave to stand overnight.

RAMBUTANS (Ngoh)

These fruits are so popular and such an important crop that the Thais dedicate a special day to the rambutan in August. It looks a little like a sweet chestnut, but with a hairy, red, green, yellow or even orange skin, depending on the variety. The flesh of the rambutan, which surrounds a large stone (pit), is a translucent white with a sweet flavour. The sweetest variety is the rongrian. Rambutans keep for up to a week in the refrigerator.

LYCHEES (Lin-chi)

Another import from China, there are about 20 different varieties of lychee cultivated in Thailand and they are an important export crop. The knobbly, reddish, brittle skin encloses a white, juicy flesh that is slightly fibrous. In the centre of the fruit is a large mahogany-coloured shiny seed. Lychees have a wonderfully scented aroma and a flavour similar to that of muscat grapes; they make a refreshing end to a meal.

LONGANS (Lamyai)

This is closely related to the lychee and the flesh has a similar appearance and texture, though less pronounced flavour. Longans are small and round with a light brown, brittle skin. When they are in season, clusters of the little brown fruits are piled up by the roadside, ready to be sold by vendors. Buy fruit on the stalk, if possible, and check that the skins have no defects. Because of their very high sugar content, the fruits go off quite quickly.

ABOVE: *Rambutans have a distinctive skin covered in soft spiky hairs.*

ABOVE: *Lychees have a sweet, scented flavour that is similar to muscat grapes.*

LANGSATS AND DUKUS (Langsat and long gong)

Both fruits are egg-shaped and grow in bunches. The duku is slightly larger than the langsat, with a thicker skin. The flesh of both fruits is white, but in some varieties of duku it may be pink. The taste ranges from sour to sweet, and it is juicy and refreshing. Both fruits can be eaten raw.

MANGOSTEENS (Mangkhut)

These are quite small, about the size of a plum, with a thick, deep purple skin that encloses segments of creamy, pink-veined flesh. The flesh is very sweet, and has a sharp, scented flavour, suggestive of peaches.

PASSION FRUIT (Saowarot)

The fruits of the passion flower vine have been cultivated in Thailand for only 60 years. They are about the same size as a plum. The leathery skin is either brown or yellowish orange. Inside are edible dark seeds in a sweet jelly-like pulp with a lemony tang. In Thailand passion fruit juice is a popular drink. The seeds are eaten, too, usually with a sprinkling of salt.

CUSTARD APPLES (Noina)

Originally from Latin America, custard apples, also known as cherimoyas, were introduced to Thailand some 300 years ago. Externally the fruit looks like a small cluster of tightly packed green grapes. When ripe, the flesh of the custard apple is sweet and creamy, which is how the fruit acquired its name. Custard apples are used in ices, drinks and desserts.

ROSE APPLES (Chomphu)

Thailand has several different varieties of this fruit, which is also known as the water apple. It is prized for its thirst-quenching nature, rather than for the flavour, which tends to be rather bland. Rose apples are seldom sold outside their native land.

ABOVE: *The bright yellow star fruits are also known as carambolas.*

STAR FRUIT (Mafuang)

Also known as carambolas, the star fruit is a bright yellow fruit with a bland, slightly sharp flavour. The fruit has a waxy-looking skin that forms five lobes or "fins", which, when cut widthways, make star-shaped slices. These make an excellent garnish for fish or poultry. They are available in supermarkets and Asian stores.

PITAYA (Gaew mungkorn)

Also known as dragon fruit, these are very pretty. About 10cm/4in long, they have bright pink or yellow skin, covered with green-tipped scales. The flesh, which is white, and speckled with tiny, edible seeds, tastes rather like melon and the seeds add an interesting crunch. This fruit is best when eaten chilled.

ABOVE: *Sapodillas have a dull, matt skin, but inside is a wonderfully sweet, flavoursome flesh.*

SAPODILLAS (Lamut)

About the same size as a kiwi fruit and similar in texture, albeit with a browny orange skin, the sapodilla has sweet flesh with a honey/caramel flavour. Peel the fruit with a knife, then use the knife tip to flick out the inedible seeds from the flesh. The Thais enjoy sapodillas with a squeeze of lime juice as a dessert fruit.

JUJUBES (Phutsa)

These fruits are about the same size and shape as plums. They have green, shiny skin, slightly mottled with sienna. Beneath the skin, which is edible, is crisp, white flesh surrounding a single, large stone (pit). The flavour resembles that of an unripe pear: sweet, yet with a hint of sharpness.

SWEET TAMARIND (Makman wan)

This bean-like fruit has irregular pods 7.5–15cm/3–6in in length. Inside these, the flesh is white and sweet, with a number of brown seeds. When young, the fruit is eaten in Thailand, usually with a spicy dipping sauce.

LIMES (Manao)

These small green and very sour citrus fruits are used extensively throughout Thailand. Thin slices of lime may be used as a counterbalance to very sweet fruits, such as mango and papaya. Fresh lime juice is highly valued as a drink, served with salt and sugar, and is also used in salad dressings.

Kaffir Limes (Makrut)

These have almost no juice but their aromatic rind is grated and used in numerous savoury dishes. Kaffir lime leaves are an essential flavouring in Thai cooking. They have a lemony fragrance and are shredded and added to soups, fish and chicken dishes. Buy unblemished, unwrinkled specimens.

ABOVE: *Limes are a very popular flavouring in Thai cooking.*

ORANGES (Som tra)

In Thailand, two main varieties of orange are available: the sweet orange, with a green/orange skin and sweet, juicy yellow or orange flesh; and the tangerine, with its easily separated segments of sweet, slightly tart flesh. Store at room temperature.

POMELOS (Som-o)

The largest member of the citrus family, a single pomelo can weigh as much as 1kg/2¼lb. Several varieties are grown in Thailand, but the most popular, because of their sweetness, are the khao hom and the thongdi. Like papaya, pomelo is a popular breakfast fruit and it is also paired with spicy dishes.

PINEAPPLES (Sapparot)

In Thailand, there are two main varieties: the phuket with its brownish-yellow skin and sweet flesh, and the pattawia, a larger fruit which is dark green and not quite so sweet. The raw fruit and the juice are popular but pineapple is also used cooked.

ABOVE: *Pineapples are an important crop and are used in cooking and eaten raw.*

ABOVE: *Watermelon has a high water content, making it very refreshing.*

WATERMELONS (Taeng mo)

The juicy flesh of this large, round fruit is very refreshing. The thick green rind and pink flesh make it a popular fruit for carving and it may be the feature on a banquet table.

DURIANS (Thurian)

These huge fruits can weigh as much as 10kg/22lb. The khaki green skin is covered with fat spikes. Inside is firm yellow flesh surrounding large seeds. Its unpleasant, pungent smell has been likened to that of raw sewage or over-ripe blue cheese. Despite the smell, locals regard the durian as an aphrodisiac. The variety called mon tong is the best. The flavour of the flesh is exquisite and most people find that once they start eating the fruit the smell is no longer a problem.

JACKFRUITS (Khanun)

In appearance, jackfruits resemble durians although they are less spiky. The creamy, succulent flesh has a sweet taste, somewhat resembling pineapple and banana. It is excellent served with ice cream.

COCONUTS

The palms on which coconuts grow can be found throughout South-east Asia. They fringe the golden beaches, surround villages, palaces and temples.

Coconuts are a very important resource for the Thais. The palm fronds are woven into mats or baskets or used as simple roofing material; the fibrous outer husks can be used as fuel or made into mats or ropes; the hard shell can be used as a drinking vessel or made into a utensil. The milk can be drunk or used in curries and desserts, and the nut can be eaten or made into oil.

ABOVE: *Coconut is amazingly versatile.*

Making coconut cream or milk

1 Chop the flesh from a coconut finely. Place in a bowl and pour over hot water. Steep for 10 minutes.

2 Strain the coconut mixture through a fine sieve (strainer) lined with muslin (cheesecloth).

3 Squeeze out any remaining liquid. This will produce creamy milk. For coconut cream, let the liquid settle. The cream will rise to the surface and can be skimmed off.

Fish

Thailand is a country blessed with an abundance of fish. In the northern part of the country, most of it comes from freshwater sources – canals, rivers, paddy fields, lakes and ponds. Along the coast, there are vast numbers of different fish to be caught, from red snapper to mackerel and sea bass.

Thai fish is prepared in several ways, depending on the type. Meaty fish is usually fried with lots of pepper and garlic or chilli sauce; sometimes it is wrapped in a banana leaf and either grilled (broiled) or barbecued (grilled); and the more delicately fleshed fish are often steamed with chillies, lime juice and other aromatic ingredients.

FRESHWATER FISH

Several varieties of fish feature in Thai cooking and are to be found in the inland waterways of Thailand.

Catfish (Pla doog)

The common catfish is about 30cm/12in long. It is very widely distributed throughout the north of Thailand. A favourite way of cooking it is to deep-fry pieces until crisp, then stir-fry them with a spicy chilli paste and other ingredients. Catfish is also used in curries and as the basis of a hot-and-sour salad called yum pla doong foo. In addition to the common catfish, there is a slightly smaller

BELOW: *Catfish is so-named because it appears to have "whiskers" on its face.*

version – pla boo – which is usually steamed and served whole in soy sauce or lime juice.

Tilapia (Pla nin)

This popular and appetizing fish is farmed throughout Thailand. A mature fish weighs about 500g/1¼lb. One of the most popular restaurant dishes using tilapia is pla nin towd rad prig, where the fish is deep-fried and then served in a slightly sweet sauce flavoured with mild chillies. Tilapia is also used in the pungent Thai curry called kaeng som, and sometimes you will find haw mok pla nin, a spicy but flavourful dish where the fish is

mixed with condiments and coconut milk and steamed in a banana leaf. Another popular method of cooking tilapia is to fry the skin. The scales are first removed and the skin is cut into short narrow strips and then deep-fried. It is served as finger food, often seasoned with lime juice or a slice of onion.

Serpent head fish (Pla chorn)

This is a fierce-looking fish with a mouth full of sharp teeth. During the rainy season, farmers may catch large serpent head fish in the shallow waters of their paddy fields. The flesh is rather bland, but it takes on the seasonings of the dish. Serpent head fish is famously used in pla chorn pae za, when it is steamed before being served in soup stock, with lime juice and salted plums. It is also used in the soup tom yam.

ABOVE: *Tilapia has firm white flesh with an extremely good flavour.*

Grey fish (Pla grai)

This is a bony, grey-coloured fish about 60cm/24in long with pronounced "eye" markings in its soft underbelly. The flesh is very soft and is usually removed from the bone and mixed with chillies and other seasonings before being formed into fish cakes. The cakes are deep-fried and served with a sweet, spicy dipping sauce as an appetizer or snack.

Trout (Pla wan)

Although trout is not indigenous to Thailand this delicate and mild-flavoured fish is regarded as a sophisticated alternative to local freshwater varieties. The Thais cook trout in a variety of different ways, but one of the most popular methods is to deep-fry the fish and serve it with a strong chilli sauce – pla nuea orn.

SEA FISH

Off the coast of Thailand, in the Indian Ocean to the south-east and the Gulf to the west of the southern peninsula, there are enormous numbers of all kinds of sea fish.

Mackerel (Pla to)

This small oily fish is very popular in the markets, where it is often displayed on rattan trays. For nam prig pla tu, the steamed fish is pounded in a mortar with curry

paste and hot chillies to make a chilli sauce. Mackerel is also steamed or fried with a chilli paste flavoured with shrimp paste.

Salted mackerel is dried and packed in oil. It has a very salty taste but a small amount of fried salted mackerel, sprinkled with chilli, sliced shallots and lime juice, makes a perfect accompaniment to a rice dish.

Sea bass (Pla krapang khan)

This versatile fish has a fine-flavoured firm white flesh that is suited to most cooking methods. The soft delicate flesh of this fish makes it ideal for steaming. An excellent way to do this is to first marinate the whole fish in aromatic spices and wrap it in a banana leaf before cooking it over coals.

RIGHT: Sea bass is an ideal fish for cooking whole, and it is excellent wrapped in a banana leaf and then steamed.

ABOVE: White pomfret has tender, fine-flavoured flesh that divides easily into fillets and is ideal for steaming.

Red snapper (Pla krapong daeng)

More than 250 species of snapper are found in the warm seas around the world and the red-skinned variety eaten in Thailand is found in the Indian Ocean. In Thai markets, red snapper is usually sold as fillets, because it is so bony. It is generally either steamed "Chinese-style" with lime juice or soy sauce, or deep-fried and covered with chillies, or combined with a coconut-based curry paste.

White pomfret (Pla jaramed)

This small silvery-skinned fish is shaped like a crescent moon and has a curved forked tail. The fish is 30–50cm/12–20in in length. It has very few scales and no pelvic fins, making it easy to clean. The firm texture of the flesh makes this fish ideal for steaming with aromatic ingredients such as ginger. It can be prepared like red snapper, or fried and covered with curry sauce or other spicy sauces.

Shellfish

The coastal waters that surround Thailand are a wonderful source of shellfish of all types, from prawns (shrimp) to mussels, clams, crayfish, lobsters, squid and scallops. Crabs are eaten with tremendous relish, whether they come from the sea or from fresh water.

PRAWNS/SHRIMP (Gung foi)

Prawns are abundantly used in Thai cooking, whether grilled (broiled), added to a tom yam soup, curried, stir-fried with tamarind or served satay-style. Fermented shrimp are used to make a paste and dried shrimp are also an important ingredient.

Deveining and peeling prawns

This is a simple technique. Once mastered, it will speed up your preparation of prawns considerably.

1 Twist off and remove the head, then slice off the tip of the tail. With both thumbs, pull the shell apart from beneath, then discard it, with the legs.

2 With a sharp knife, make a tiny incision down the back of each prawn.

3 Using the tip of the knife or a pair of tweezers, carefully remove the black intestinal cord from the back of the prawn. Rinse the shelled prawn under cold running water and pat it dry before cooking.

ABOVE LEFT: *Raw prawns vary in colour, from shades of grey to orange and red.*

BELOW LEFT: *Prawns turn pink on cooking whatever their size, variety and original colour.*

Shrimp balls (Look chin bla)

Shrimp balls can be used in soups or curries, grilled (broiled), cooked on the barbecue or deep-fried.

They are made from puréed shrimps and flavoured with garlic and Thai fish sauce. The mixture is formed into balls and cooked for a few minutes in boiling water. They will keep for about 1 day in the refrigerator, or can be frozen for up to 3 months.

Butterflied prawns

This attractive way to prepare prawns also speeds up the cooking process.

1 Remove the heads and shells of the prawns but leave the tails intact. Slit the backs and devein.

2 Make a cut through the underside of each prawn without cutting all the way through, then open out the two halves so that they look like wings.

ABOVE: *Mussels and clams are often combined in a Thai dish.*

MUSSELS, CLAMS AND OYSTERS (Hoi malang puu, hoi, hoi naang rom)

Mussels and clams frequently feature on the Thai menu. They are served together in a popular dish flavoured with lemon grass and coconut cream. Mussels steamed with Thai herbs is another simple but very successful speciality. Oysters are often used with other shellfish to make a seafood salad. They are blanched in boiling water, then drained and tossed in a spicy dressing with fresh herbs.

Preparing mussels

When buying mussels or other bivalves such as clams or oysters, make sure they come from unpolluted waters. If the mussels have been farmed, you will probably not need to purge them to rid them of sand, but if you have harvested the mussels yourself, clean them thoroughly, then soak them for several hours in a bucket of water to which you have added a little flour or oatmeal.

Check the mussels to make sure that the shells are tightly closed. Any mussels that remain open should shut immediately if you tap them. If they don't, throw them away because they are dead. Scrub the shells thoroughly and pull off the hairy "beards".

To open the shells, place the mussels in a pan with a small amount of boiling liquid. Steam gently for 3–5 minutes. Remove the mussels when the shells open, discarding any that remain resolutely shut. If you prefer, the mussels can be opened in the oven. Place them on a baking sheet and put them in a preheated oven at 150°C/300°F/Gas 2 for a few minutes. When they open, serve on the half shell, or separate the flesh from the shells with a sharp knife.

SQUID (Pla meug)

Popular in Thailand, squid is available both fresh and frozen. Squid should always be cooked very quickly; if cooked for too long it will become rubbery. It only takes about 30 seconds to cook in hot water and 1–2 minutes if stir-fried. Squid can be grilled (broiled), deep-fried, steamed or added to soups and salads.

Preparing small squid

1 Hold the body with one hand and gently pull off the head and the tentacles with the other.

2 Cut between the eyes and tentacles, taking care not to pierce the ink sacs. Discard the eyes and ink sacs. Remove and discard the small hard beak between the eyes and tentacles.

3 Place the body, fin-side down, on a board. Use your fingers or an angled knife to carefully scrape off the thin skin. Pull out the guts from inside the sac, then rub the sac inside and out with salt. Set the squid aside for about 5 minutes, then rinse off all the salt very thoroughly under cold running water.

4 Separate the tentacles and cut the longer ones in half. Pat the body and tentacles dry with kitchen paper. The body can be stuffed, using the chopped tentacles as part of the filling, or cut into rings. Alternatively, cut the body lengthways into four, score the pieces in a criss-cross pattern, then cut into strips.

LEFT: *Squid is ideal for stir-frying, as it requires only a very short cooking time.*

Poultry

Most Thais purchase their poultry live or freshly killed from the market. While this guarantees freshness, the sight of bamboo cages filled with scrawny chickens, pigeons and ducks can be daunting to the visitor.

CHICKEN (Kai)

One of the most popular meats in Thailand, the versatile flesh of a chicken suits pungent Thai spices and simple methods of cooking. It seems that every area of Thailand has its own favourite chicken curry recipe. Chicken also lends itself to other treatments, as when it is teamed with lemon grass or cashew nuts. Frying, cooking on a barbecue or brazier, or roasting are also popular methods. Stir-fried chicken with chillies and holy basil is a speciality, the rich flavour of the basil tempering the heat of the chillies. Chicken is delicious roasted with lime and sweet potatoes, and chicken cooked on a barbecue is a common sight in markets.

DUCK (Yahng)

Thai cuisine owes much to Chinese influences and nowhere is this more apparent than in the Thais' passion for duck. It is often cooked in the same ways as chicken, but some duck dishes are very elaborate. In bet yahng, the duck is marinated in a mixture of honey, soy sauce, bean sauce, chilli, garlic and vinegar, then roasted on a spit until the skin is crisp.

The skin is then removed and served with rice and the partly cooked meat is used in a stir-fry. Duck meat is also often cut into bitesize pieces and marinated with flavourings such as five-spice powder, sesame oil and orange rind and juice, then cooked with coconut milk to make a hot and spicy curry, or chopped and stir-fried with chilli and Thai fish sauce.

Cutting up a chicken

This method produces eight portions. If you need more pieces the portions can be further divided. Accomplished Thai cooks will be able to cut the breast and wing portions into as many as 10 pieces.

1 Place the chicken breast-side up. Ease one leg away from the body. Make an incision to reveal the ball of the thigh bone as you pull the leg away from the body. Once the thigh socket is visible, cut through it to release the drumstick and thigh in one piece. Repeat with the other leg.

3 Using a large sharp knife, a pair of poultry shears or strong, sharp scissors, cut through the breastbone, starting at the neck end. Cut and separate each breast and wing portion from the backbone, carefully cutting through the wishbone with a pair of shears or scissors, then trim off any flaps of skin.

2 Trim off the end of the leg bone, then turn the leg upside down and locate the knee joint. Cut the leg in half, cutting through the joint. Repeat with the other leg.

4 Cut both wing and breast pieces into two portions each, slicing through the meat and bone. Make stock from the bones, adding onion, celery, ginger or lemon grass.

Meat

Although rice, noodles and vegetables form the major part of the Thai diet, Thais are not, in general, vegetarians. Pork is the meat of choice, except for Muslims, who do not eat pork for religious reasons – beef or lamb is usually eaten instead.

PORK (Mu)

This meat is enormously popular and every part of the pig is eaten. Pork is very versatile and can be combined with practically all Thai ingredients. Many of the pork dishes illustrate the Chinese influence in Thai cuisine, including barbecue-spiced pork and sweet-and-sour pork. For stir-frying, fillet, lean leg and belly (side) are the preferred cuts, while for stews and braised dishes, belly pork is used.

Pork belly (Mu sam chan)

This is the same cut of pork that is used for making bacon, with a layer of red meat, fat and skin. Pork belly is regarded as one of the tastiest cuts of the animal despite its fatty content and it is a particular favourite, whether fried until crisp or slowly cooked with five-spice powder. The long cooking method makes the pork particularly tender and also helps render much of its excess fat. Cooked this way it is often served with plain boiled rice and vegetables. Pork belly is often used minced (ground) with other meats or fish to provide flavour and moistness. It is often combined

ABOVE: *Pork belly is a popular cut for frying and for snacks.*

with prawns (shrimp) in prawn cakes and also with beef to give added flavour to Thai meat balls.

Pork skin (Nang mu)

Simply boiled, or boiled and then deep-fried, pork skin is a Thai speciality. It is made by removing all the hair and fat from the skin, which is then scraped clean, boiled until tender, then sliced. Frozen pork skin is sold in Asian stores.

BEEF (Neua wua)

Until fairly recently, beef was rarely eaten in Thailand as cattle were highly valued for their work. Today, beef is still relatively expensive, so is used sparingly. Beef is generally cut into bitesize pieces. For stir-frying, it is first sliced along the grain, then across the grain into thin slices. Beef is also grilled (broiled), stewed, minced (ground) and stir-fried, or made into meatballs, and served as satay.

LAMB (Neua gae)

Although not as popular as pork or beef, lamb is used in some classic Asian dishes, particularly those originating in Muslim areas.

Making crispy belly of pork

This popular snack is not unlike pork scratchings.

MAKES ABOUT 675G/1½LB

1kg/2¼lb belly (side) of pork
120ml/4fl oz/½ cup Thai coconut vinegar
60ml/4 tbsp salt
sunflower oil, for deep-frying

1 Score the skin on the belly of pork crossways with a sharp knife. Brush the skin with the vinegar and leave to dry. Repeat three times, then rub the pork skin with the salt.

2 Cut the pork crossways into thin strips. Spread out on a baking tray and cook in a preheated oven at 120°C/250°F/Gas ½ for about 3 hours until completely dry.

3 Heat the oil in a wok and deep-fry the pork in batches for 5 minutes, until the skin has crackled and is golden.

Herbs, spices and aromatics

One of the distinguishing features of Thai cuisine is the way in which a combination of flavourings is used to achieve precisely the desired taste in a dish. Try to use the specified item wherever possible; if this isn't always possible, there are acceptable substitutes.

BASIL

There are three types of basil grown in Thailand, each one with a slightly different appearance, flavour and use.

Thai basil (Bai horapa)

The most important of the three basils, Thai basil has a sweet, anise flavour and is used in red curries. It looks similar to the Western sweet basil except that it has purple stems. Sweet basil can be used instead.

Holy basil (Bai grapao)

This variety tastes rather like cloves, which explains its alternative name: hot basil. The leaves release their full flavour when cooked. Use as fresh as possible, in fish dishes and curries.

Lemon basil (Bai manglaek)

This herb does not travel well, so you are not likely to encounter it outside Asia. It looks a little like Italian dwarf basil, and the Thais use it in soups and sprinkle it over salads.

Bay (Bai grawan)

Although the Thai bay leaf is not the same as Western bay, both belong to the same family and have a similar flavour. Thai bay leaves are used in Mussaman curry and soups.

CARDAMOMS (Luk grawan)

These have a warm, pungent flavour. Cardomoms consist of small pods – about 1cm/$\frac{1}{2}$in – which contain tiny, slightly sticky black seeds. Green cardamoms are the best. Cardamoms are used in both savoury and sweet dishes. In Thailand, it is one of the flavourings for Mussaman curry.

CHILLIES (Prik)

The Portuguese introduced chillies into Thai cooking in the 16th century. Before that, black pepper was used to give dishes a hot, spicy flavour. There are hundreds of varieties of chilli. As a rule, the smaller the chilli, the hotter the flavour, but there are exceptions.

Bird's eye chillies (Prik kee noo)

Small and very hot, these popular chillies are used in curries as well as pickles, soups and sauces.

Long chillies (Prik chee fa)

Known as cayenne chillies and used for the eponymous spice powder, these may be red, yellow or green.

Dried red chillies (Prig hang)

A huge range of dried chillies are used in Thai cooking and they are available from Asian stores either in packages or strung together.

Chilli powder (Prig kee nu bonn)

This is made from ground dried red chillies, sometimes with additional spices. The strength varies but Thai chilli powder is invariably very hot.

CORIANDER/CILANTRO (Pak chee)

The entire coriander plant is used in Thai cooking. Each part, whether roots, stems, leaves or seeds, has its own unique flavour and specific use. The fresh, delicate leaves are used in

BELOW: *Tiny bird's eye chillies are thin-fleshed and fiery hot.*

ABOVE: *Coriander is a versatile herb, and Thai cooks use every part from the leaves and seeds to the roots.*

sauces, curries and for garnishes, the roots and stems are crushed and used for marinades, and the seeds (which may be toasted) are ground to add flavour to curry pastes.

SAW LEAF HERB (Pak chii farang)

Also known as the sawtooth herb, this takes its name from the appearance of the leaves, which are long, slender and serrated. The herb has a similar but rather more pungent flavour than the coriander leaf. Saw leaf herb is used as a flavouring for meat dishes.

CUMIN (Mellet yira)

The whole seeds of this aromatic spice are not used individually in Thai cooking (though they are in other Asian cuisines, such as Indian), but ground cumin is an important ingredient in curry pastes such as krung gaeng.

PREPARING CHILLIES

Always wash your hands thoroughly with soap and water immediately after handling chillies. The volatile oils can cause extreme stinging if placed near your eyes or face and other sensitive parts of your body.

Preparing fresh chillies

Using a sharp knife, remove the stalks and halve the chillies lengthways. Scrape out the pith and seeds, then slice, shred or chop the flesh as required. Either discard the seeds or add to the dish, depending on the amount of heat required.

Preparing dried chillies

1 Remove the stems and seeds with a knife, then leave the dried flesh whole or cut into 2–3 pieces. Put the chillies in a bowl, cover with hot water and leave to soak for 30 minutes.

2 Drain, reserving the soaking water if it can be added to the dish. Use the chillies as they are, or chop finely.

Making chilli flowers

Thai cooks are famous for their beautiful presentation, and often garnish platters with chilli flowers.

1 Holding each chilli by the stem, slit it in half lengthways. Keeping the stem end of the chilli intact, carefully cut it lengthways into fine strips.

2 Put the chillies in a large bowl of iced water, cover and chill in the refrigerator for several hours. The cut strips will curl back to resemble the petals of a flower. Drain the flowers well, then use to garnish dishes. Small chillies may be extremely hot, so don't be tempted to eat the garnish.

ABOVE: *Galangal, which comes in both dried and fresh forms, is similar in flavour and appearance to ginger.*

GALANGAL (Kah or laos)

This rhizome is a member of the ginger family and is used in a similar way. When young, the flavour is lemony, and it is best used in soups. As it matures, the flavour intensifies and it is used in curry pastes.

Lesser galangal (Krachai)

Also referred to as lesser ginger, this rhizome has a flavour that is a cross between ginger and black pepper and is most often used in jungle curries and with fish. Peel and prepare it in the same way as ginger.

GARLIC (Kratiem)

With coriander (cilantro) root and black pepper, garlic makes up the famous Thai seasoning trio. The Thais use huge amounts of garlic in their

Deep-fried garlic

This is delicious sprinkled on top of soups and salads. Peel garlic cloves, slice and deep-fry them over a medium heat, stirring until light golden. Remove with a slotted spoon and transfer to kitchen paper.

cooking. Thai garlic tends to be smaller and more pungent than garlic in the West.

GINGER (Khing)

In Thailand there are several different types of ginger. The roots are used medicinally and for flavouring food. Common – or King – ginger is the best-known variety. Fresh root ginger is widely available from supermarkets.

JASMINE (Malee horm)

Also known as Arabian Jasmine, it is the basis of jasmine extract – yod nam malee. The buds are soaked in water overnight, and the water is then used to flavour cakes and desserts, such as perfumed rice. Jasmine extract can be bought in bottles, but the commercial product lacks the subtlety of fresh jasmine water.

LEMON GRASS (Takrai)

Widely available fresh in Asian stores and supermarkets, this is an essential ingredient in Thai cooking. The citrus flavoured plant is used in curries and hot-and-sour soups.

BELOW: *Mint is often used in Thai cooking, especially in salads.*

Preparing fresh root ginger

Fresh root ginger is peeled before being used for cooking. The dry thin skin is easy to peel using a small sharp knife. You can then slice the flesh thinly, cut it into fine slivers, chop it or grate it. If fresh root ginger is to be discarded after cooking and used purely as a flavouring it should be lightly bruised, using a flat knife.

MINT (Bai saranee)

Mint is a popular herb in Thailand. The leaves are often used fresh in salad.

PANDAN LEAF (Bai toey hom)

Leaves from this fragrant member of the Pandanus or screwpine family are long and slender, and look a bit like a whisk broom. Pandan leaves have a slightly woody, nutty taste. They are used as a wrapping for pieces of chicken or pork and also as a flavouring for cakes.

PEPPERCORNS (Prik Thai)

Before chillies arrived in Thailand, pepper was the major spice to provide the heat for Thai food. Thai cooks use two types of peppercorns: white for seasoning and green as a garnish for curries and stir-fries.

TAMARIND (Mak-kaam)

One of the main souring agents in Thai cooking, tamarind is fruity and refreshing and has a tart and sour flavour without being bitter. It is an essential ingredient of Thai hot-and-sour soups. In Thailand fresh tamarind is widely available, but in the West you are more likely to encounter it in a compressed block. Lemon juice can be used instead.

FENNEL SEEDS (Yira)

When ground, these warm, aromatic seeds are one of the ingredients of five-spice powder, a Chinese ingredient that is popular in Thailand.

TURMERIC (Kamin)

Related to ginger and arrowroot, this rhizome is a bright orange-yellow inside. It can stain the skin, so some people wear gloves when preparing the fresh root. When cut it has a peppery aroma and it imparts a slightly musky flavour to food. In Thailand it often forms part of curry pastes, especially those of Indian origin, and is used to colour rice.

BELOW: *Turmeric is most often sold ready ground in the West, but the fresh root is sometimes available.*

CURRY PASTES AND POWDERS

Most Thai curries are based on "wet" spice mixtures, pastes produced by grinding spices and aromatics in a heavy mortar with a rough surface.

Red curry paste (Krung gaeng ped)

This paste gets its colour from the large number of fresh red chillies that are the prime ingredient. Red curry paste is most often used in beef curries and robust chicken dishes.

Green curry paste (Krung gaeng keo wan)

This curry paste is made from herbs and fresh green chillies. It is most often used to make chicken curries.

Orange curry paste (Krung gaeng som)

Made from red chillies and flavoured with shrimp paste, this tangy paste is often used in seafood curries, including sour shrimp curry soup.

Yellow curry paste (Krung gaeng karee)

Similar to Mussaman curry paste, a quick version can be made by adding a generous amount of turmeric to red curry paste. It is very spicy and is used for chicken and beef curries.

Mussaman curry paste (Nam prig gang Mussaman)

This curry paste owes its origins to India. It is based on dried chillies and contains coriander and cumin.

Penang curry paste (Nam prig gang panang)

This sweet curry paste is made with ground roasted peanuts and is relatively mild.

Curry powder (Pong gka-ree)

When curry powder is used, it tends to be in a stir-fry, marinades or a peanut sauce.

Making a curry paste

It may be more effort than using a food processor, but preparing curry paste in the traditional Thai way with a mortar and pestle will produce better results. Use a gentle pounding action, softening the larger ingredients before blending the mixture together. This will preserve all the subtle aromas, and ensure that the flavours are well integrated. Unused paste can be stored in the refrigerator for a week.

ABOVE: *Green and red curry pastes – the first step to many Thai curries.*

Storecupboard ingredients

It is always worth keeping a stock of oils, vinegars, pastes and sauces in your storecupboard – these are all Thai staples.

OILS (Naam man)
Nowadays, light vegetable oils are used in Thai cooking.

Groundnut/peanut oil
The advantage of using this oil is that it can be heated to a high temperature without smoking.

Corn oil
This is good for deep-frying, but it is less suitable for dressings, where its strong flavour dominates.

Safflower and sunflower oils
Both these oils are lighter in taste than groundnut or corn oil, but they are slightly less suitable for stir-frying.

ABOVE: *Sesame oil and chilli oil are used for seasoning rather than for cooking and are generally added to dishes just before serving.*

Soya oil
This is used for general cooking, but is not appropriate for use in salad dressings.

Sesame oil
Seldom used for frying because it burns easily, sesame oil has a strong nutty flavour. It is frequently used as a seasoning oil, sprinkled over food just before serving.

Chilli oil
This spicy oil is never used in cooking, but is used as a dipping sauce.

RIGHT:
Amber and white rice vinegars have a distinctive sharpness.

VINEGARS
Rice vinegar (Nam som sai chu)
This white vinegar is made from fermented rice grain and has a sharp clean taste which is milder than the Chinese or Japanese versions.

Coconut vinegar (Nam som maplow)
This opaque liquid has a fruity aroma and a sweet and sour flavour that is typically Thai.

ABOVE: *Chilli bean paste should be used with caution, as it is very hot.*

SAUCES AND PASTES
Chilli sauce (Saus prik)
Made from chillies, water, vinegar, sugar and salt, this comes in several intensities as regards heat and sweetness. The sweeter varieties go well with chicken or seafood.

Sriracha sauce (Nam jim Sriracha)
Named after the seaside town where it originated, this sweet-tart, hot or mild bottled table sauce is made from red chillies.

Thai fish sauce (Nam pla)
One of the most important ingredients in Thai cuisine, fish sauce is made from salted fish, usually anchovies, which are fermented to create the thin liquid that is the basis of the sauce.

Soy sauce (Namm see ewe and namm see ewe sai)
Two basic types of soy sauce are used in Thai cooking: salty and sweet. There are two versions of the saltier sauce. One is light coloured while the other is darker and thicker. The sweeter sauce comes in two strengths. One is thin and the other, which has been

processed with molasses, is thicker. Both are used with the salty soy sauce in noodle dishes or stir-fries.

Oyster sauce (Hoy nangrom)

Thick and dark brown, its principal ingredients are soy sauce and oyster extract. It has a distinctive taste which, strangely, is not at all fishy.

Chilli paste (Nam prik)

This is the most popular condiment in Thailand. It is on the table at every meal. There are many different versions of the sauce but the main ingredients are chopped red chillies – with the seeds – fresh lime juice, shrimp paste, Thai fish sauce, garlic and a little sugar.

Chilli bean paste (Naam prik pao)

This is made from soya beans, chillies and other seasoning. The paste is very hot. It is sold in airtight jars.

Magic paste (Prig gang nam ya)

This commercial product is sold in Asian stores. It is a blend of garlic, coriander (cilantro) and white pepper and is used a lot in Thai cooking.

Shrimp paste (Kapee)

One of the most widely used ingredients in the Thai kitchen, this paste has a powerful flavour. There are many types of kapee, varying in colour from pink to dark brown. The pink one is good for curry paste, the darker one for making dipping sauces.

ABOVE: *Palm sugar, sometimes called jaggery, is dark brown, moist and unrefined. It has a distinctive, but extremely delicate flavour.*

DRY INGREDIENTS
Agar agar (Sarai talay)

This setting agent, made from seaweed, is used instead of gelatine in Thailand.

Palm sugar/jaggery (Nam taan peep)

Made from the sap of the coconut palm or the sugar palm tree, this is less sweet than cane sugar. It is often sold as a solid cake that needs to be grated. Use soft brown sugar as an alternative.

Tapioca (Meun)

Made from the tubers of the cassava plant, pearl-shaped pieces of tapioca are used in desserts, giving them a gelatinous consistency. Tapioca flour is used for thickening sauces, making batters and coating foods for frying.

Toasted rice powder (Khao kua pon)

This seasoning and binding agent is pale brown with a nutty flavour and is used with minced (ground) shrimp or meat for kebabs, sprinkled on soups and tossed with meat for salads.

NUTS AND SEEDS
Lotus seeds (Med bua)

Fresh lotus seeds are eaten as a snack food, and puréed and mixed with sugar to make a filling for cakes. The dried seeds must be soaked in water before use. Remove the green shoot in the centre of each seed before use. The seeds are prized for their texture and ability to absorb other flavours. They are often added to soups. Look for dried lotus seeds in Asian stores.

Peanuts (Tua lii song)

Often roasted and used extensively as a garnish, peanuts also add texture to salads. Chopped, they form the base for satay sauce and thick red curries and they are also the main ingredient of Penang curry paste.

Sesame seeds (Ngaa)

These tiny seeds are usually white, but can be cream to brown, red or black. Raw sesame seeds have very little aroma and flavour until they are roasted or dry-fried, which brings out their distinctive nutty flavour and aroma.

ABOVE: *Skinned, raw and whole peanuts are widely used in Thai cooking. They also form the base for satay sauce.*

Equipment

You can produce authentic Thai food at home with just a few simple pieces of kitchen equipment.

MORTAR AND PESTLE (Krok and saak)

The most important piece of equipment in any Thai kitchen is without a doubt the mortar and pestle. Ideally, it would be good to have a selection of different sizes or at least two, one for grinding spices and the other for making salads. They are made of granite, earthenware or wood. Buy one that has a capacity of at least 450ml/³⁄₄ pint/scant 2 cups and is about 18cm/7in in diameter. The granite mortar and pestle are ideal for grinding spices and herbs whereas the earthenware and wooden ones are usually used for the less robust method of making salads.

Some people use a coffee grinder (kept specially for the purpose), or a blender or food processor for grinding their spices and

herbs, but none of these produces the authentic texture or flavour that the traditional method achieves.

To remove any pungent odour or staining from your equipment, soak in a mixture of distilled vinegar and water for about an hour, and then rinse out. If, as is likely, chillies have been ground, a mixture of salt and lime juice can be used to clean the equipment.

WOK (Kata)

Following closely on the heels of the mortar and pestle's prime position on the kitchen shelf is the wok, a versatile cooking vessel that can be used for stir-frying, deep-frying, roasting or steaming. The wide, sloping shape of the wok makes it efficient to cook in and easy to use.

Woks are available in different materials: spun carbon steel, stainless steel or aluminium. The best material is spun carbon steel. There are non-stick versions made with a special coating, but they do not conduct the heat as efficiently as the traditional ones and they also cannot be heated to such high temperatures. If you have a gas stove, a round-based wok is best. If your stove is electric, then you will have to use a flat-based wok. A wok stand is used to help keep the wok steady on the hob (stovetop). It is very helpful if you want to use the wok for steaming, deep-frying or braising.

LEFT: A granite mortar and pestle is useful for making the traditional Thai "wet" spice pastes.

ABOVE: *Woks may have flat or rounded bases and one or two handles.*

The light, domed wok lid, used for steaming, is available from Asian stores. If you are unable to find one, any lid that fits tightly will do.

Seasoning a wok

Woks that are not non-stick need to be seasoned before you can use them. When new, they should be thoroughly washed to remove the machine oil that protects them during their transportation. Scrub the inside with a cream cleaner, then rinse and dry with kitchen paper. Place the wok over a very low heat and add 30ml/2 tbsp cooking oil, rubbing it all over the inside with kitchen paper. Continue heating the wok gently for a further 10–15 minutes, then wipe it again with a thick pad of kitchen paper, protecting your fingers. Repeat the process until the paper comes away clean.

FINE KNIFE (Miit)

This thin knife is used for peeling and carving fruit and vegetables into decorative shapes.

ABOVE: *A Chinese cleaver (right) is finely balanced and a bamboo grater (left) is useful for grating fresh root ginger.*

UTILITY KNIFE (Li-toh)

A hardy, hatchet-like utility knife can be used for splitting coconut shells and chopping wood for kindling.

CHINESE CLEAVER (Miit muu)

This is a versatile piece of equipment. A cleaver is used for chopping through bones and also for cutting delicate slices for stir-frying. It must always be kept razor sharp. Alternatively, a large heavy chef's knife can be used.

SOUP SERVER (Tao fai)

A soup server can be made of aluminium, tin-lined copper or brass. They are sometimes referred to as Mongolian hot pots. Always make sure that the soup server has a non-corrodible lining such as tin.

GRATER (Tsota-drap)

Bamboo graters are ideal for grating ginger, while a stainless steel box grater is useful for shredding vegetables and grating coconut flesh for milk.

Traditionally coconut was prepared using a special grater – *maew khuut ma-phroat*. These are now more collectors' items rather than everyday kitchen utensils.

What were once plain, small stools with sharp metal graters set into one end have evolved into elaborate pieces of equipment.

To use the traditional coconut grater, the chef sits astride the seat, holding the halved coconut against the grater. Beginning at the outside rim and working towards the centre, the coconut is grated to different thicknesses. Today electric graters and hand-held metal graters are used.

CURVED SPATULA (Phai)

This long-handled, curved wooden spatula is an essential tool for stir-frying in a wok.

STEAMERS (Huat)

The traditional Thai steamer – *huat* – is a set of bamboo trays, stacked over a wok of boiling water with a cover on top. Chinese merchants introduced perforated metal pans which are used in the same way. Electric steamers are also widely used today.

ABOVE: *Stacking bamboo steamers are used in a wok of boiling water.*

To prevent the food from sticking to the steamer while cooking, banana leaves, damp muslin (cheesecloth) or baking parchment may be placed under the food. Before using a bamboo steamer for the first time, wash and rinse it and then steam empty for at least 5 minutes.

A special round, flat steamer – *rang theung* – made of steel or bamboo is used for steaming delicate fish, dumplings, desserts or other dishes.

CHOPPING BOARD (Khiang)

A traditional Thai chopping board is round, about 5cm/2in thick and made from tamarind wood. Any hard wood or acrylic board would be suitable, as they are easy to clean, hygienic and will last for a long time.

Never place food that is not going to be cooked (such as salads or cooked foods) on a board where raw meat or poultry has been cut. Use a separate board for raw meat, and keep it clean.

SIEVE/STRAINER (Kra-chawn)

You will need a selection of different size sieves for straining different items, from rice to juices and oils.

METAL BATTER MOULDS (Krasthongs)

These shell-shaped brass moulds are set on the end of a long wooden handle. The mould is dipped first into hot oil, then batter, and then back into the oil, where it cooks to form crisp little cups. These cups are filled with savoury mixtures and are served as snacks called krathon.

Basic cooking techniques

Careful preparation is the foundation of all Thai cooking, from chopping ingredients to grinding spices and trimming garnishes. Once the ingredients are prepared, then the cooking can commence.

The most important component in Thai cooking is the spices and herbs, which give dishes their unique flavour. It follows that getting these prepared correctly will ensure you get the best possible results from your cooking.

GRINDING SPICES

The ideal method for grinding spices is to use a large Asian-style mortar. The rough sides tend to "grip" the spices, stopping them flying out of the mortar as you pound them.

1 Cook the spices over a high heat for 1 minute, shaking the pan. Lower the heat and cook for a few more minutes, until they start to colour.

2 Transfer the toasted spices to the mortar and pound to a fine powder to release the essential oils.

POUNDING AND PURÉEING

Dry and wet spices, aromatics and herbs are often pounded together to form spice pastes. Other flavouring ingredients such as strong-tasting shrimp paste may also be added.

1 Place the spices, herbs and any other flavouring ingredients in a mortar and pound with a pestle for a few minutes to form a smooth paste.

SLOW-COOKING

Stewing *(keang)* is the typical method for preparing Thai soups and curries, and the very lengthy cooking time means that meats are very tender. Traditionally, a heavy clay pot would have been used.

Put all the ingredients in a clay pot and place in an oven preheated to the required temperature. (A heavy casserole makes a good alternative. If flameproof, it can also be placed over a medium heat on the stovetop.)

STEAMING

This is an excellent way of preparing delicate foods such as fish and vegetables. Steaming *(neung)* helps to retain the flavour of ingredients and keeps them intact.

1 Place the food in a bamboo steamer. (Some recipes require the steamer to be lined with banana leaves.) Put the steamer on a wok rack over a wok half-filled with boiling water. Steam the food, replenishing the water constantly to prevent it boiling dry.

2 Parcels of food wrapped in banana leaves can also produce steamed results. Place a well-sealed parcel over a barbecue or in a preheated oven. The moisture is trapped within the parcel and steams the food inside.

BOILING

This method *(dom)* is often used to cook delicate meat such as chicken breast portions or duck.

Place the meat and any flavourings in a pan and add just enough water to cover. Bring to the boil, then leave to stand, covered, for 10 minutes. Drain.

STIR-FRYING

This is a very quick cooking method – it is the preparation of the ingredients that takes time. Prepare all the ingredients before you start to stir-fry *(pad)*. The order in which ingredients are added to the pan is very important.

1 Pour a little oil into a wok and place over a high heat for a few minutes.

2 Add spices and aromatics to the wok and stir-fry for a few moments.

3 Add pieces of meat, poultry, fish or shellfish to the wok and stir-fry for 2 minutes, shaking the pan constantly.

4 Add any hardy vegetables such as carrots, green beans or (bell) peppers and stir-fry for 1 minute.

5 Add any delicate vegetables and leaves such as beansprouts, spinach or morning glory and stir-fry for about 1 minute more.

6 Add more seasoning and any fresh herbs such as basil or coriander (cilantro) that should not be cooked for long. Toss to combine and serve.

DEEP-FRYING

This method *(tord)* is used for many dishes such as wontons, spring rolls and prawn crackers. Use an oil that can be heated to a high temperature, such as groundnut (peanut) oil.

1 Pour the oil into a deep pan or wok and heat to 180°C/350°F. To test the temperature, add a little batter or bit of onion. If it sinks, the oil is not hot enough. If it sizzles and rises to the surface, the temperature is perfect.

2 Cook the food in small batches until crisp and lift out with a slotted spoon when cooked. Drain on a wire rack lined with kitchen paper and serve immediately, or keep warm in the oven until ready to serve.

COOKING ON THE BARBECUE

Grilling *(yarng)* food over glowing coals is very popular. It is widely used by street vendors, who cook skewered snacks such as satay or barbecue-cooked chicken (kai yang) or seafood over small open braziers.

1 When using charcoal, light the coals and wait until they are covered with a layer of white ash before starting to cook. Place the food on a rack over the coals and grill until cooked.

2 If using a barbecue is not convenient, cook the food under a preheated grill (broiler).

Wooden and bamboo skewers

If you are using wooden or bamboo skewers, soak them in water for about 30 minutes before using to prevent them from burning.

Index